Philosophy of Educational Research

Second Edition

Also available:

Reflective Practice in Educational Research Linda Evans

Quantitative Methods in Educational Research Stephen Gorard

Educational Research in Practice Joanna Swann and John Pratt

Doing Qualitative Research Geoffrey Walford

Educational Research Jerry Wellington

Continuum Research Methods Series
Series Editor: Richard Andrews

Research Questions Richard Andrews

Evaluation Methods in Research Judith Bennett

Analysing Media Texts Andrew Burn and David Parker

Action Research Patrick Costello

Ethics in Research Ian Gregory

Researching Post-compulsory Education Jill Jameson and Yvonne Hillier

Systematic Reviews Carol Torgerson

Real World Research Series

Developing a Questionnaire Bill Gillham

The Research Interview Bill Gillham

Case Study Research Methods Bill Gillham

Philosophy of
Educational Research

Second Edition

Richard Pring

continuum
LONDON • NEW YORK

Continuum

The Tower Building
11 York Road
London SE1 7NX, UK

15 East 26th Street
New York 10010
USA

www.continuumbooks.com

First published 2000
Reprinted 2001, 2003
Second edition 2004
Reprinted 2005

British Library Cataloguing-in-Publication Data
A catalogue record for this book is available from the British Library.

ISBN 0–8264–7261–3 (paperback)

Typeset by YHT Ltd, London
Printed in Great Britain by CPI Bath

Contents

To Faye

Preface to Second Edition

This second edition has changed a little, partly as a result of criticisms, partly because of certain gaps in the previous account, and partly because I needed to reflect upon the nature of the activity I was engaged in – the practice of philosophy about education and in particular about doing research in education. In this, as indeed in the early part of the book, I have benefited from reading and re-reading papers by Professor Wilfred Carr (see, particularly, Carr, 2003). My own view of 'doing philosophy' has, of course, its own presuppositions, and these need to be made explicit and subjected to critical examination. But it is precisely this reflexive intelligence which should be at the heart of all professional practice – working, certainly, within the rules and understandings of a given practice, but reflecting upon the nature of these rules and understandings so they might be improved or adapted to new and previously unseen situations. Practical philosophy in that sense is a particular kind of deliberation.

On the other hand, although philosophy about education (and in particular about research activities within it) will be different in different places and eras, nonetheless there are perennial issues and themes which transcend such differences and which make such practical deliberations eventually philosophical. Such issues and questions concern the nature and accessibility of knowledge, what it means to be and behave 'as a person', the basis of the values we think worth pursuing, the relationship between mind and body and between the individual and society. Such issues, though constantly reformulated, will ever remain central to our thinking about education and about the conduct and interpretation of research.

—1—

Setting the scene: criticisms of educational research

There is a great deal of educational research. In the USA, the annual cost of both federal and state funding is over a billion dollars. In the 2001 Research Assessment Exercise in the United Kingdom, the names of 2045 academics were submitted as active researchers – 800 less than in 1996. The grading of their research became extremely important because of the funding consequences – many universities were, as a result, much poorer. Despite such poverty for some, the annual spending of public money upon educational research cannot be far short of £100 million (see Hargreaves, 1996, footnote 1, and 1997).

On the other hand, many believe that this money is not well spent, and this was reflected in Britain in the 'Hillage Report' (1998) (hereafter 'Hillage') sponsored by the Department for Education and Employment. First, research does not provide the answers to the questions government asks in order to decide between alternative policies on, say, class size or school organization or the provision of nursery education. Second, research does not help professional practice in such matters as the teaching of reading or pupil grouping or teaching methods. Third, research is fragmented – lots of bits and pieces which, though often addressing similar questions, start from different positions or use different samples, not creating a coherent and reliable basis for practice or policy. Fourth, research is often tendentious or politically motivated – and exclusive of those who do not share the ideological underpinnings of the research programme (see Tooley and Darby, 1998).

Such criticisms were emerging in the political arena some years before. This is illustrated by the contribution of Lord Skidelsky to the debate in the House of Lords concerning the proposal to transfer responsibility from the Higher Education Funding Council to the Teacher Training Agency for the funding of educational research.

Many of the fruits of that research I would describe as an uncontrolled growth of theory, an excessive emphasis on what is called the context in which teaching takes place, which is code for class, gender and ethnic issues, and an extreme paucity of testable hypotheses about what works and does not work. (Quoted by Bassey, 1995, p. 33, together with his excellent response in the *Times Educational Supplement*)

This sceptical attitude towards research is by no means confined to teachers and policy-makers – or, indeed, to Britain. The criticism has been made within the educational research community itself. Hargreaves (1996), drawing upon a North American critique of educational research and his own Leverhulme funded research, argued that, despite the enormous amount of money spent on research and the large number of people who claim to be active researchers, there is not the cumulative body of relevant knowledge which would enable teaching to be (like medicine) a research-based profession. For it to be so, it would be necessary to change, first, the content of that research, and, second, the control and sponsorship of it. Content would need to focus on the practice of teaching and learning – to build up sufficient, well-tested bodies of knowledge to serve as guidelines for professional practice in, say, the teaching of reading or in the grouping of pupils in classrooms. Of course, such a corpus of knowledge would be complex and would need to be used flexibly because situations, context and personalities of both teacher and learner affect the relevance of research statements. None the less, such a research exercise would seem possible. Teachers would need to be involved (as doctors are in the development of research-based medicine) in identifying the research needs, in formulating the questions which respond to these needs and in collecting the data – to make it 'rooted ... firmly in the day-to-day professional practices ...'. The relationship between 'professional researchers', as it were, and teachers would be very different – much more integrated in the setting of agendas and in the undertaking of the research. This is, of course, reiterating what Stenhouse (1975, chapter 10) had argued, namely, that only the teachers could appreciate, and have access to, the complexity of data required to understand the interactions of the classroom.

As Hargreaves demonstrates by his references, the concern about the quality and the relevance of educational research is by no means a peculiarly British phenomenon. Lortie (1975) is quoted as saying

Teaching has not been subjected to the sustained, empirical and practice-oriented inquiry into problems and alternatives which we find in university based professions ... [T]o an astonishing degree the beginner in teaching must start afresh, uninformed about prior solutions and alternative approaches to recurring problems ...

More recently, the issues have been thoroughly discussed in the pages of *Educational Researcher* (see Slavin 2002). Carl Kaestle (1993) asked the question, 'Why is the reputation of educational research so awful?'. In a collection of papers addressing these matters, Goodlad puts the problem bluntly:

Criticism of educational research and statements regarding its unworthiness are commonplace in the halls of power and commerce, in the public marketplace, and even among large numbers of educators who work in our schools. Indeed, there is considerable advocacy for the elimination of the locus of most educational research – namely, schools, colleges and departments of education. (In Berliner *et al.*, 1997, p. 13)

But the reasons seem to lie not so much in the lack of an adequate knowledge-base. Indeed, Gage dismisses those critics who say that research has not provided the well-tested generalizations which can inform practice. But he does take the researchers to task for their failure to develop an adequate theoretical framework within which well-established research might be brought to bear upon educational understanding and practice. There is a need for the 'meta-analyses' of existing research to meet the needs of those who want to know the evidence for supporting one policy rather than another, or one educational practice rather than an alternative (Cooley *et al.*, 1997). Berliner draws a similar conclusion: there is the body of knowledge, but it is not synthesized in a way which can relate to teachers' administrators and politicians.

Scriven, however, is much more censorious, declaring that educational research 'does not in itself make a contribution to what I have called educational research's "principal duty to the society"'. Indeed, using once again the medical reference which we are now accustomed to,

If medical research had only contributed explanations of disease but had neither identified nor developed any successful treatments, we would surely say that it had failed in its principal duty. (Cooley *et al.*, 1997, p. 20)

The debate is best summarized by Kennedy's (1997) contribution, referred to by Hillage. This gives four reasons for the failure of research to have an impact upon educational practice: its seeming irrelevance to practice, its poor quality as compared with research in other fields (particularly the social sciences), its inaccessibility, and the incapacity of the educational system itself to think and make decisions on the basis of research.

This United States debate is summed up by Lagemann (1999, p. 3) as follows:

It has to be acknowledged that studies of education tend to 'get no respect'. Indeed, no other areas of scholarship have ever been more scorned and demeaned. Educational research has been accused of ignoring important questions while reinforcing practices that stand in the way of fundamental reform. It has never been a professionally dominated field of study and as a discipline has been internally fragmented.

The consequences of these criticisms are of two kinds. On the one hand, research is dismissed as worthless, not deserving funding. Its quality and relevance are challenged. With its own peculiar language (often technical, abstract and obscure), the research is seen to have gone adrift from the complex, but common sense and practical world of education. On the other hand, though not altogether worthless, research is seen to need greater external control so that it is made to serve the purposes and answer the questions of the non-research community – politicians, administrators and teachers. Indeed, money has already been shifted in Britain from universities to teachers via the Teacher Training Agency, so that the Agency or the teachers can determine the research which is professionally relevant and, indeed, conduct it themselves. And, as a result of such criticisms, there are initiatives, both in the UK and in North America, to learn from the developments in evidence-based health care and, through systematic reviews of research (especially randomized controlled tests) to answer specific policy and professional questions by reference to well-established evidence (see the series of papers in Thomas and Pring, 2004).

To answer these criticisms would require a detailed account of research over the years and an analysis of its impact upon policy and practice (see Kirst and Ravitch, 1991, for illustration of United States policies which have changed as a result of research, and Edwards, 2000, for similar examples from Britain). As Hammersley (1997) argues, there is a danger in looking for too direct a relation between research conclusions and specific rules for successful practice. Human beings (and the social life in which they interact) are not the sort of things where there can be simple causal relationships between specific interventions and subsequent behaviours. And this affects the possibility of 'cumulative knowledge'. Again, the impact of research may be indirect, a gradual shifting of public and professional consciousness in the light of growing evidence, rather than a direct relation of conclusions to practical decisions; research into the performance of girls at school in specific subjects would be an instance of that. On the other hand, the impact has been direct in certain policy decisions such as in the establishment of Educational Priority Areas, following the research of Halsey on the relation of educational performance to social conditions (see Halsey, 1972). A more recent example would be the effect of research about school effectiveness on both policy and practice, beginning with the Rutter Report (1979) and Mortimore and Sammons (1997) and also Mortimore (1999). One might also cite the way in which research entered into major curriculum development projects, shaping their direction and thereby influencing rather than determining the practice of the teachers. Examples would be the research into the influential Humanities Curriculum Project or Nuffield Science (see Elliott and MacDonald, 1975).

None the less, for all research which is successful in the sense that it is carried out impartially, validly and reliably and affects policy and practice, there is much which fails to impress or to have impact upon policy and practice. Of course, part of that failure might be due to the inability or unwillingness of teachers or policy-makers to heed the findings of research (see, for example, Hillage, pp. 49, 50), and there is a need to see how research might enter into the thinking and decision-making of those who work within the education system. Or it may be that research challenges valued assumptions or favourite policies and for that reason is ignored or rejected.

However, it would be wrong for educational researchers to resort to such defences too quickly. Maybe there is a lot of bad research. And one reason for poor quality might be that, conceptually and philosophically, the research simply does not make sense. Indeed, it is a surprising fact that so much educational research espouses controversial philosophical positions without any recognition of the philosophical problems which they raise and which often have been well rehearsed by philosophers from Plato onwards. No wonder there is a suspicion of researchers when there is an appeal to 'the social construction of knowledge' or to 'the multiple realities of the learner' or to 'subjective meanings of the learners' or to 'the personal construct of truth'. So much flies in the face of common sense understandings of the problem and its solution. And as the researchers embrace with enthusiasm and uncritically the latest 'ism' (such as 'postmodernism') so the gulf between researcher and teacher is even more unbridgeable.

First, therefore, philosophical examination of research questions, and of the enquiries to which those questions lead, must start by trying to get clear the nature of that which is to be researched into. The nature of the subject matter determines what kind of research is valid or relevant. Or at least, the nature of that which is to be researched into will determine the relevance of different sorts of research and their findings. In the case of *educational* research it is important to attend to what is distinctive of an *educational practice*. There may be important differences as well as similarities between education and, say, medicine (with which Hargreaves draws a comparison) which imposes certain logical limits on how far the one research tradition can be transferred to the other (for example, in the application of randomized control trials).

Second, depending on the nature of that which is being enquired into, the model of the social science research, in which there is conceivably a cumulative body of knowledge, may or may not be appropriate.

Third, the gulf, which creates a barrier to the dissemination of research, between the language of teachers (whose practice research must ultimately relate to) and the technical language of the researcher, may be the fault of researchers – cut adrift from the common sense language of those who practise.

These issues – the nature of *educational* enquiry, the model of *social science* in its changing forms, and the links between the *language and concepts* of research and those of practice – will be the constant themes of this book. They raise some of the most central problems of philosophy – of the *meaning* of what is stated, of the *truth* of what is claimed, of the *verification* of conclusions reached, of the *conceptualization* of a problem and its solution, of the *objectivity* of enquiry and of the *knowability* of reality – although this too often remains unacknowledged by researchers or treated in the cavalier manner which brings that research into disrepute. In a nutshell, many of the problems to which Hargreaves points are, at base, philosophical and need to be recognized as such.

The term 'research' is used to refer to any 'systematic, critical and self-critical enquiry which aims to contribute to the advancement of knowledge' (see Stenhouse, 1975, p. 156). It is broad enough to encompass not only empirical research, but also historical, documentary and philosophical research. One might refer here to Bassey, 1995, for a useful mapping of the different kinds and dimensions of educational research arising from the Stenhouse definition. But a much more valuable mapping of different kinds of research – and in particular of the issues and criticism associated with it – is that of Oancea (2003). Clearly, therefore, such research in its critical enquiry draws upon the social sciences, but it is the argument of this book that it cannot be reduced to them. The distinctive features of any enquiry are determined by the nature of the subject matter to be enquired into. It is part of the philosophical task both to keep the social sciences at bay and to show how and when they can be appropriately drawn upon.

The focus of educational research – educational practice and policy

THE DISTINCTIVENESS OF EDUCATIONAL RESEARCH

It is important to reflect upon what is distinctively *educational* research, if only for the practical reason that, unless there is something distinctive, then such research might be seen simply as a subset of research within the social sciences (and more effectively undertaken within those departments rather than within departments of educational studies). Of course, that might bring to educational research a rigour which too often is lacking. But it may also distance that research from what is distinctively educational – it may not be about what the 'educators' need to know. It is a question of whether the 'practice' of education can be properly understood within the language and understandings of the social sciences.

These problems seem to have emerged in the decision to close the School of Education at the University of Chicago. This School is claimed to have been one of the most prestigious centres of educational studies and research in the world. It succeeded the Department of Pedagogy, founded by John Dewey in 1894 together with the Laboratory School, where Dewey's influential views on education and teaching were developed and tested out. It was there that Dewey questioned the 'dualisms' between theory and practice and between thinking and doing as a basis of 'intelligent action' arising from a systematic reflection upon the 'problems to be solved' (see Dewey, 1916). Sadly, by not heeding the programme of Dewey, the School had disconnected its theoretical pursuits from the practice of school teaching whilst failing to produce the research which met the academic approval of the social scientists. This surely is a lesson for all those who, in pursuit of academic excellence, neglect the relevance to practice. Indeed, it is this distancing of theory from practice which was seen by those who contributed to the debate in *Educational Researcher* as a major cause of the public scepticism about educational research.

I want to draw a distinction between research which is firmly embedded within the social sciences and which may well be relevant to education, and research which arises from distinctively educational concerns and which draws upon, but is not to be reduced to, the knowledge which has accumulated within those sciences. The distinction may sometimes be blurred and it may be that educationally relevant research may often be properly placed in the disciplines of psychology, sociology or philosophy. But it can only be relevant if it relates to the 'practice of education' – to the activities, engaged in on the whole by teachers, which have those characteristics which pick them out as *educational*.

All activities can be seen and understood from different perspectives. And educational activities can no doubt be understood from non-educational perspectives, depending on the questions being asked. Thus, a social psychologist might provide interesting observations on what he or she sees in the classroom, which may not be relevant to the *educational* understanding of what is happening.

Before enlarging on this point, I want to say something about defining or clarifying a concept like 'education'.

DEFINING WHAT WE MEAN

One might think that research should begin with clarifying what is being researched into, and thus with a definition of key terms. Disagreement between people is often a disagreement over the meaning of the words being used. Once they have been clarified, then often the source of disagreement disappears. Ambiguity is to be avoided.

However, clarifying or defining terms is a controversial matter – especially terms like 'education' which might be described as 'essentially contestable'. By that I mean that certain words can rarely be defined in a way that attracts universal agreement. The reason is very often that they embody values which themselves are contestable within society. There are different views about what is to count as an 'educated person', and there is no obvious way in which these differences might be resolved.

There are various ways of getting around this problem. The first is to *stipulate*, in precise and unambiguous terms, what you mean when you use a particular word. For example, to be educated might be said to *mean* to be able to read, to write, to be acquainted with and appreciate a certain literature, etc. There are many examples of the use of *stipulative definitions* in recent educational discourse, as government and its agencies set clear and unambiguous standards against which teachers, schools and colleges are held accountable. Definitions of 'competent teacher' by those who accredit teacher training courses, or of 'intelligence' by educational psychologists in terms of scores on intelligence tests, are examples of that. However, language, and our understanding of the physical and social world through that language, are not like that. Concepts (through which experience is organized), and the words which embody and express those concepts, can be grasped only within a system of concepts (or within a language). Their meaning lies partly in the logical interconnections with other concepts. Thus, the way in which we apply the word 'intelligent' is too rich and complex to be reduced to the stipulative definitions which suit psychological researchers. Recognition of this complex conceptual and language structure makes nonsense of stipulative definitions, as readers of *Alice in Wonderland* will recognize.

Second, of course, there are *ostensive definitions* – where a word is defined by pointing to the objects to which it exclusively refers. Thus, in defining 'education', one might point to particular activities or to what goes on in particular schools. And, indeed, that is what so often happens. Examples of good practice, pointed to by politicians or inspectors, are used to *show* what education is – and means. But that is unacceptable because one wants to know by what characteristics these different activities are picked out as examples of 'education'. What does this label signify that 'indoctrination' or 'training' does not?

Third, however, definitions are not confined to ostensive or stipulative ones. Getting at the meaning of a word requires close examination of its *usage* – the complex logical interconnections entailed by its use in different contexts. After all, the meaning of a word is its use in a language with *agreement* not only in its definition in terms of other words but also in its application to experience. How else could communication be intelligible? Therefore, we think hard about what is implied in our description of someone as 'educated' or in calling an activity or experience 'educational'. What logically follows from such a description? What kind of evidence would make one withdraw one's judgement? Would it make sense, for example, to call the process of learning *educational* where there is clear evidence of indoctrination?

A fourth approach, especially where ordinary usage leaves things open (where, for example, there are differences of view about the application of a word), is to think of the different ways of understanding which are brought together under this one label. That requires the patient unravelling of these understandings. For example, there is criticism of 'child-centred education'. 'It' has been blamed for poor standards in schools, and some research claims to have demonstrated as much (Bennett, 1976). But there is no stable usage of this term. It points to different sorts of practice. A useful philosophical job, therefore, is to trace the different traditions associated with this description. One needs to show how these different traditions embody different views about the nature of knowledge, the point and value of education, and the respect due to the child. There are different child-centred traditions, embodied in different metaphors – the biological one of likening the child to a growing plant (Froebel) or the more socio-biological one of Dewey, who talks of the importance of the 'experiential continuum' between the child and its environment (see Dewey, 1936). Research which lumps these together for empirical enquiry fails to see important differences which are relevant to how the enquiry is conducted, the data collected and the conclusions drawn.

It is important, therefore, in researching anything, to attend to the 'logic of the discourse' of that which is researched into – in this case, 'education'. By that I mean the rules implicit in the use of particular words and those to which they are logically related. The ways of describing and evaluating activities as 'educational' incorporate a particular mode of conceptualizing and valuing experience. There are implicit assumptions about what sorts of experience should be described as educational and what sorts of people should be regarded as educated.

But it soon becomes clear that there are important differences between people in how the word is applied – albeit within a broad area of agreement about its definition. To that extent its meaning is contestable. That is because the concept of education implies a set of values, and there is disagreement over what those values are. One person might regard an appreciation of music essential to the 'educated person'. Another might attach little importance to such appreciation but stress an understanding of sciences. Yet another might emphasize practical wisdom associated with experience. The Dearing Report (1994) in Britain proposed that the humanities and the arts should no longer be part of the compulsory National

Curriculum after the age of 14. No argument was forthcoming why priority should be given to science and mathematics. But this was clearly an *educational* judgement.

Therefore, in researching education we are engaged in two sorts of clarification – first, the general usage of the term (which is complex enough) and, second, the different ways in which the term is applied, especially in its evaluative sense, depending on different traditions of what is considered to be of value. For example, Muslims press for opportunities for an Islamic education, and an Islamic understanding of education including science (see *Muslim Education Quarterly* for a series of papers on the islamization of the teaching of English and science); there is a strong tradition within the Catholic Church of a distinctively Christian understanding of education (see Maritain 1937 and 1943, and Carr, Haldane, McLaughlin and Pring 1995). At one level (purely conceptual), education means roughly the same; at another it assumes different sets of values, different ways of seeing the world. Beware those who, ignoring these conceptual points, speak with confidence about what their empirical investigations demonstrate. It all depends on what you mean.

THE CONCEPT OF EDUCATION

What then is it for an activity to be distinctively educational?

Dewey (1916) distinguished between educational and *mis*educational activities. Those activities were educational which led to further 'growth'. A miseducational activity or experience was something which blocked growth. However important, *objectively speaking*, a lesson or curriculum might be judged, if it turned pupils off or closed minds to further thoughts or dulled the sensibility, then it was not educational. Boredom was the 'mortal sin'; 'growth', 'problem-solving', 'enrichment of experience' ('experiential continuum') and 'intelligent action' the key concepts. For Dewey, therefore, education concerned the development of the distinctively human capacities of 'knowing', 'understanding', 'judging', 'behaving intelligently'. Miseducation, by contrast, referred to whatever stunted the development of such capacities.

Let me expand on this. What distinguishes human beings, according to Dewey, is their capacity to adapt to new situations and experiences, not as other organisms simply through biological adaptation, but through conceptualizing problems and possible solutions. Every problem is a 'forked-road situation' – alternative possibilities are identified and tested out. If the hypothesis proves to be correct, then a particular way of thinking is confirmed and strengthened. But that results in further questions, further problems to be solved. There is no end to this expanding, growing way of understanding, adjusting and questioning in the light of experience, enquiry and criticism. Education is concerned with the life of the mind, and such a life can atrophy if not carefully nurtured. The job of the teacher is to facilitate that development through putting the learner in contact with further experience or with what others have said (in literature, say) as they make sense of similar experiences. Education takes place within a community of learners, where that community includes previous generations who have contributed to the public understandings upon which each individual draws in trying to make sense of the world. And the expertise of the teacher lies in being able to inhabit both the world of the learner and the world of public understandings, and thereby to establish the 'continuum' between them. There is both a public growth of understanding and a personal one, and education lies in the interaction between the two.

Dewey illustrated several important features of 'education'. First, the concept is primarily *adjectival* and *evaluative* – it picks out activities and experiences because they meet certain evaluative standards. The concept does not name specific activities as intrinsically educational – learning of Greek verbs, knowledge of historical dates, acquisition of scientific facts. Any activity or experience can be educational; it depends on the *quality of the experience* which it gives rise to. Second, the particular quality of experience lies in the *kind of learning* which takes place. Does it help to make sense of things – to give a clearer and more fruitful way of conceiving the problem and its possible solutions? Does it lead the learners to ask further questions, to open further lines of enquiry, to engage more fruitfully with the experiences confronting them? The educated person has a lively and questioning mind, though disciplined by what others have said on such matters.

The meaning of 'education', therefore, might be characterized as follows:

First, it refers to those activities which bring about learning. Hence, we talk about educational systems or institutions established with the specific purpose of getting people (particularly young people) to learn. Educational research, therefore, must focus upon learning. At the centre of learning lies the development of what Peters (1965) referred to as 'cognitive perspective' – those structures of the mind or conceptual framework through which experience is understood, organized and made sense of. Without a broader cognitive perspective (that is, with only a partial and limited vision), one would have a distorted perception of reality. Hence the complexity of educational research because it is not clear what, in every case, counts as a person having learnt or having understood something, let alone having attained the mental qualities which are educationally valued.

Second, however, not any kind of learning is regarded as educational. 'Education' picks out those learning activities which are, from some point of view, regarded as worthwhile. (This point is disputed by, for example, Wilson, 1979, p. 27; but he does not pay sufficient attention to the idea of the 'educated person' both historically and in ordinary usage or political argument.) Of course, different people will have different views of what is worth learning, and thus of what counts as a 'good education' or an 'educated person'. And that creates complications for educational research – for example, in international comparisons of educational achievement or in judgements about educational standards, because standards are logically related to the values held. For Dewey, worthwhile learning was that which was 'fruitful' in enabling people to adapt successfully to new situations and to identify (and deal with) problems as they arise. 'Education' referred to experiences or instructions which nurtured the capacities (the concepts and skills, the mental operations and dispositions) for subsequent problem-solving and enquiry. There will be disagreement over what these capacities are, and such a disagreement will partly be ethical. 'What knowledge is of most worth?' asked Herbert Spencer, and the history of education is characterized as much by ethical debate over what kind of knowledge is to be valued as it is by anything else. Or, to put it in a slightly different way, as Bruner notes in his excellent 'Postscript' to Lagemann and Shuman's (1999) *Issues in Educational Research*: 'Education – and education research – cannot be kept separate from the life of the culture at large' (p. 408).

Third, what is worthwhile learning, in an educational sense, depends on its contribution to the development of someone as a person. We learn many things, even useful things, which leave untouched the deeper feelings and ways of understanding and appreciating. It is as though the learning is 'skin-deep' – stuck on, as it were, with sticky tape. Such learning can easily be discarded, and this would make little difference to the person concerned. But education refers to that learning which in some way transforms how people see and value things, how they understand and make sense of experience, how they can identify and solve key problems. Educational experiences do not leave people as they were. People become, in an important sense, different *persons*.

I am not talking about anything dramatic. To grasp a basic concept in biology such as 'osmosis' opens up a new and more informed way of seeing the growing, physical world; the appreciation of a war poem by Wilfred Owen sensitizes one to the horrors of war. Most societies, therefore, would have some idea (or, indeed, several and possibly competing ideas) of the transforming qualities, attitudes, skills, knowledge and understandings which help create the more fully developed and 'educated person'. It is difficult, therefore, to think about education, let alone about research into it, without addressing questions about the qualities which constitute or lead to a worthwhile form of life. And that question in turn requires careful examination of what it means to be a person and to be so more fully. It is one of the absurdities of much research into the 'effective school' that these issues are ignored. 'Effective schools' are those which produce specific outcomes. But there is rarely any explanation why *these* outcomes are constituents of a worthwhile form of life, or whether the process through which the outcomes are produced transforms the learner in a significant way.

Fourth, as a development of the above point, there remains a close connection between the learning that is attained and the process through which it is attained. Education points to a distinctively human mode of acquiring the understandings, beliefs, attitudes and skills which we would want to identify with the educated person. There is an *attempt* to make sense, a *process* of enquiry, a *questioning* of solutions, an *adaptation* of frameworks of understanding to new challenges, a *making personal* the 'solutions' offered in an *impersonal* form. Hence, education is generally understood to exclude 'indoctrination' or 'conditioning'. It respects the personal commitment to understanding and making sense of experience, recognizing that such a commitment will shape people in different ways – certainly not producing the standardized outcomes loved by some researchers.

Fifth, although one talks about 'educated by experience', it would be difficult not to see 'teaching' as an essential element in the normal educational process. Certainly, education can take place in many kinds of informal setting. One might be educated by experience or through wise nurturing by family, community and workplace. It makes sense, too, to talk of educating oneself. Educational research, therefore, might with profit look at such informal modes of education. But, first of all, there are limits to how far such informal approaches can really introduce young people into the understandings, skills and knowledge which need to be acquired for living in a modern society or for gaining access to the riches of the culture which we have inherited. Furthermore, it is precisely because such informal settings are inadequate for these purposes that learning is deliberately organized, that institutions are created, and that people are employed professionally as teachers, in order to initiate the next generation into these forms of understanding, skill and knowledge. And the teaching or the transactions between teachers and learners within an educational practice cannot be disconnected from that institutional framework with the embedded beliefs about the values worth pursuing. A 'practice' is more than an isolated action or activity. It is a set of activities united in a shared set of purposes and values. It is a social event in which individuals share and participate. Teaching is required to mediate the *public* knowledge and traditions of thought and criticism to the *personal* questionings of the young person trying to enter into that public world. Otherwise that transforming experience of education would be extremely limited. Far from growing as a person, each would be locked into his or her own private world.

To summarize, education refers to those activities, on the whole formally planned and taught, which bring about learning. Hence, we talk about a person being educated at such and such a school or university. But the evaluative sense of the word implies that the learning is worthwhile. It is so because it contributes to personal well-being, providing the knowledge, understanding and values which enable people to think in the way that is considered worthwhile and to live their lives more fully. Training in a particular skill may or may not be educational, depending on the extent to which it opens up the mind and contributes to that growth as a person. Put like that, one can see why there are inevitably disagreements in society over what precisely a good education should consist of. People disagree about the qualities which make someone more fully a person, or what knowledge, in this day and age, is important, or what skills one needs to be trained in. Is the knowledge demanded by the National Curriculum really necessary for a fully human form of life? What questions should people be asking about the environment, say, or about moral issues concerning race or gender? What knowledge and skills are needed for answering them?

Such a characterization of education highlights the kind of enquiry or research needed to shed light on educational activities and their assessment and evaluation. Such enquiry cannot avoid the ethical dimension to education, the different ways in which people – teachers, the wider community and the learners themselves – find value in some experiences and activities rather than others. Such an enquiry must focus upon the quality of learning which takes place – not only what is learnt but the manner in which the learning occurs. Furthermore, the research cannot escape from examining how that learning transforms the learner. By extension, the research must focus on the relationship between teacher and learner, since access to the accumulated knowledge and understandings available to the young learner cannot be attained by accident or gratuitously – that is why, as Ryan (1997) argues, Dewey is a prime example of teacher-centred education.

This view of education, and thus of educational research, is contestable. Certainly, there are logical features of the general usage of 'education', namely, its concern for learning and the evaluation of that learning as in some sense worthwhile. But not everyone would include, within its meaning, 'development *as a person*'. Here we are moving into the territory of the fourth kind of definition outlined above. I am calling upon a particular tradition of educational thinking in which education refers to those practices which, through the development of understanding and rational capacities, constitute a distinctively human form of life. Such a tradition can be neglected in a culture which fails to address questions about what is distinctively human, or which sees learning to be useful (or not) by reference to some further end or goal. In that respect, research into the 'effective school' is quite 'technicist' and utilitarian, concerned with the means and not with the value of the 'ends' to which those means lead – and not with the deeper effects upon the learner as a developing young person.

KEY CONCEPTS IN EDUCATION

Central to educational research, therefore, is the attempt to make sense of the activities, policies and institutions which, through the organization of learning, help to transform the capacities of people to live a fuller and more distinctively human life. Such research needs to attend to what is distinctive of *being a person* – and of being one in a more developed sense. It needs to recognize that the 'what' and the 'how' of *learning* those distinctively human capacities and understandings are by no means simple – they need to be analysed carefully. And *a fortiori 'teaching'*, through which that learning is brought about, will reflect that complexity.

Persons and personal development

Education nurtures the distinctively human qualities and capacities, particularly those concerned with knowledge and understanding. But what are the qualities and capacities associated with being a person?

First, the concept of person presupposes a form of consciousness, a capacity to experience the world, not merely to interact physically with it. That consciousness is shaped by different forms of understanding. These can be ever more refined through learning. Indeed, education aims to introduce the growing mind to forms of understanding which transform and make more intelligible one's view of the world.

Second, one aspect of that understanding of the world is the recognition of other people as *persons* – that is, as centres of consciousness in their own right with the capacity to think, to feel and to experience in the light of those thoughts. It is to have the capacity, too, to reflect upon oneself as a person – able to have one's own thoughts and point of view.

Third, a person with such understandings has the capacity to relate to other persons in a distinctive way – not only as one physical object to another but as one centre of consciousness to another. Persons share a world of meanings, not just a physical world of space and time.

Fourth, persons share with each other practical understandings, concerning what one should do and the ends to be served. Such deliberations assume that one can exercise control over one's own life and that one can act autonomously, not being totally under the power of others or of natural forces.

Fifth, however, the quality of personal life depends on social relationships and the institutional arrangements which support them. But these social networks and institutional arrangements, so important in the shaping of oneself as a person, are the product of human endeavour. Responsibility for one's own life extends to responsibility for the social context of that life, and that requires the dispositions, skills and knowledge to take an active part. In that sense, persons are political animals – capable of shaping the social environment that affects profoundly the quality of life.

Sixth, therefore, 'person' is a moral concept in two senses. On the one hand, it implies the capacity to take responsibility for one's own actions and one's own life. On the other hand, it indicates the desirability of being so treated – of being given the opportunity for taking on that responsibility and of respecting it in others. To be fully a person is to be held responsible for what one does and to be treated as though one is responsible. This is reflected in the moral principles of 'respect for persons' and in the moral claim to be treated with a sense of dignity.

Such a characterization of what it is to be a person stresses the various, though interrelated, capacities which may or may not be actualized through educational practice – the capacity to think and to feel, to see others as persons and to relate to them as such, to be aware of oneself as a person, to engage in the moral deliberations essential to the discharge of that responsibility, to have the ideals which uplift and motivate. But there are barriers to that exercise – ignorance, false beliefs, lack of self-respect, envy and hatred of others, absence of social skills, lack of vision to guide deliberations. And there is boredom, the failure to take interest in things around, which renders inoperative the distinctively human capacities.

The exercise of those capacities is dependent upon learning. One remains ignorant and powerless unless, through learning, one acquires the concepts and knowledge which dispel that ignorance and enable one to understand oneself and others, and one's obligations and responsibilities. Learning is essential to becoming fully a person. Through learning one acquires the ideals which ennoble and motivate, the standards by which one might evaluate one's own performances and those of others. Adolescence, in particular, is a period in which young people seek to find their distinctive identities – the sort of persons they are or might become, the ideals that are worth striving for, the qualities that they wish to be respected for, the talents that need to be developed, the kind of relationship in which they will find enrichment, the style of life that is worth pursuing.

That 'whole person' therefore requires the following, all of which depend on learning:

knowledge and understanding: the concepts, forms of thought, beliefs through which one can make sense of the world and operate intelligently within it;
intellectual virtues: honesty, not cooking the books, testing out and

sharing beliefs, openness to new ideas – but also scepticism towards untested claims;

imagination: lateral thinking, problem-solving, thinking beyond the given, making links between the present and the past, re-interpreting experience in the light of previous experiences;

intellectual skills: skills of enquiry (whether scientific in the laboratories, moral in the cut and thrust of discussion, or social in the conduct of enquiry), of reasoning, of marshalling arguments, of collecting evidence, of communicating results;

self-reflection: including the development of self-knowledge;

moral virtues and habits: such as kindness, generosity, care for the environment, sensitivity to others, humility in the face of success, courage in the face of danger, loyalty to friends – dispositions which embody ideals of how life should be lived;

social and political involvement: the capacity to participate in and to influence social activities that affect the quality of one's life;

integrity and authenticity: the capacity, amidst different demands on one's allegiance, to seek what is right and to persevere in adversity – not swayed by fashion or popularity.

Education incorporates the values which are connected with personal formation in this widest sense. But that formation is to be understood within different and competing moral traditions. Therefore, in respecting learners as persons (in respecting their integrity and authenticity) one must give them credit for the personal search for a meaningful and significant life within the range of possibilities. To engage in this search – to be authentic as opposed to taking on board passing fashions – is a daunting and often painful task. It means often the breaking with loyalties and cherished views. But it is part of the seriousness of living. And that seriousness is by no means confined to the academically able. Nor does it depend on intellectual excellence. It lies behind the voice of many who simply want to be taken seriously. In that respect, Charles Taylor refers to the 'horizons of significance' whereby each comes to see and value things in a particular way. Having such moral horizons, howsoever implicit, is essential to the deliberations and the choices over how to live one's future. He argues

> Perhaps the best way to see this is to focus on the issue that we usually describe today as the question of identity. We speak of it in these terms because the question is often spontaneously phrased by people in the form: Who am I? But this can't

necessarily be answered by giving name and genealogy. What does answer this question for us is an understanding of what is of crucial importance to us. To know who I am is a species of knowing where I stand. My identity is defined by the commitments and identifications which provide the frame or horizon within which I can try to determine from case to case what is good, or valuable, or what ought to be done, or what I endorse or oppose. In other words, it is the horizon within which I am capable of taking a stand. (Taylor, 1989, p. 27)

This gradual defining of identity is central to the task of education, and of course it will assume different forms with different people. But it has implications for the practice of education and for the nature of the transaction between teacher and learner in which are explored (critically and in the light of what others have said through literature, drama, and so on) the ideals worth pursuing, the direction in which capacities should be developed, the sort of person one should strive to become, the standards against which performance should be judged.

But does not research, employing a different language and participating in a different form of discourse, necessarily ignore this essentially moral character of education?

Learning
The central educational function of schools is to enable young people to *learn* what is valuable and significant. That then must be the defining focus of educational research.

On the other hand, one learns many different sorts of things and these differences affect the nature of research into learning and the ways in which it should be undertaken. People learn 'facts', 'concepts', 'principles', 'skills', 'attitudes', 'habits', and 'competencies'. They learn *how* to do things (for example, *how* to engage in discussion) as well as *that* something is the case (for example, *that* the chemical formula for water is H_2O) or *to* behave appropriately (for example, to work co-operatively), or to *be* someone (for example, a person of good character). The complexity of 'learning' – the logically different sorts of thing which are learnt – escapes simplistic learning theories and, thereby, models of educational research which depend on those theories or which rest too easily upon measurement or tests.

Thus to have learnt *that* something is the case requires a mastery of the concepts employed. But concepts – the way in which we organize experience – do not stand by themselves. They belong within a conceptual framework and their meaning can be grasped only within that framework – within, say, the discourse of science or economics. To have learnt a concept is to see it in relation to other concepts and to be able to apply it correctly. It is to have acquired that logical interrelation of concepts through which experience is organized in a particular way. To learn a subject, as Bruner (1960) argued, is to have mastered those key ideas and the interrelationship between them through which experience might be organized (for example, in religious understanding, 'God', 'worship', 'prayer', 'sin', 'redemption'; in classical mechanics, 'force', 'energy', 'weight', etc.).

Moreover, such ideas can be grasped at different levels of 'representation'. Learning is a 'coming to understand', a struggle to grasp the full meaning of ideas or concepts only half understood, a constant coming to deeper insight and more accurate recognition of the distinctions to be made. If learning is the main focus of educational research, then that research must attend to what it *means* to have learnt at different levels of representation. It must respect the 'logical structure' of that which is learnt – what it means to have learnt this theorem or that fact or an appreciation of that poem. To learn science is to internalize relevant concepts, forms of judgement and ways of enquiring. To get on the inside of 'doing mathematics' is to be able to use certain concepts – to apply them correctly both in identifying instances of them and in relating them to other mathematical concepts. Learning, therefore, requires a shift of consciousness whereby one comes to see things differently, proceed in a different way, and meet standards of thinking and behaving. Furthermore, such learning requires the acquisition of virtues such as a concern for the truth and openness to criticism.

It is difficult to see the validity of educational research which does not attend to this wider picture of the different kinds of learning which are characteristic of an *educational* activity. There is a danger that 'the learning society', as it is geared to the goals of economic improvement, and as it is described in management terms, will work with an impoverished notion of learning, one which fails to account for what it means to come to understand, or to see things from a different point of view, or to grasp the logical structure of a discourse, or to ponder upon and struggle with new meanings, or to reach alternative and possibly not popular conclusions. The discourse of the 'learning society' often sees things differently. Precise objectives are set and then translated into measurable behaviours, even though the logical relation between those behaviours and understanding is not explicated. Content to be learnt is prescribed even though the connection between that content and the logical structure of the subject matter is not made clear. A pace is set for covering the content as though no one needs time to ponder and to readjust. A given starting point is assumed as though there is not already a richness of understanding through which new experiences are sieved and shaped.

In sum, educational research must attend to what it *means* to learn, and that requires a careful analysis of the many different sorts of learning. Failure to do that gives rise to the kind of research which bears little relation to children's learning in schools or adults' learning after school.

Teaching

Research into 'teaching' suffers from the same problem as research into learning – namely, the reduction, for the sake of simplicity, of a complex concept to something which is easily measured. Therefore, Reynolds (1998) feels confident to say that there is a body of knowledge in effective teaching which enables us to establish guidelines on how to teach.

That is said, however, without any attempt to analyse what is meant when one claims to be teaching. An action might be described as 'teaching' if, first, it aims to bring about learning, second, it takes account of where the learner is at, and, third, it has regard for the nature of that which has to be learnt. 'Teaching habits' is different from 'teaching algebra'; 'teaching how to ride a bicycle' is different from 'teaching to be virtuous'. To disregard the nature of that which is to be taught or the readiness of the learner to learn would hardly count as teaching. It is arguable whether some so-called teaching, which disregards either the state of readiness of the learner or the nature of the subject matter, should be regarded as bad teaching or not teaching at all. Of course, there can be good teaching which does not achieve its objectives, but if it rarely achieved those objectives – if the students always failed to learn anything – then maybe the teacher has not really been teaching. The lecture on a complex scientific topic which pays no regard to the level of understanding of the audience could hardly be called teaching. Teaching is the conscious effort to bridge the gap between the state of mind of the learner and the subject matter (the public forms of knowledge and understanding) which is to be learnt, and as such the teachers' expertise lies in understanding both.

That leaves open an enormous number of activities which could count as teaching. One might teach through example, through instruction, through questioning, through structuring the classroom in a particular way, through drawing up a reading list, through preparing workshop or learning materials, through writing a textbook, or through arranging certain sorts of experiences. What makes these diverse activities *teaching* is, first, the intention to bring about learning; second, the relevance of those activities to the kind of learning to be brought about; and, third, the relevance of those activities to the state of mind and motivation of the learner. Such a connection between the purported teaching activity and the learning outcome must be one which respects the nature of that which is to be learnt. A teacher, for example, though very good in the classroom, could not be said to be teaching (as opposed to child caring) when supervising the children at swimming when he or she does not know anything about swimming. A teacher cannot be teaching physics when he does not understand the basic concepts. He may be teaching lots of things, but these things do not include physics.

Educational research, therefore, should centrally, but not exclusively, be about those transactions between teacher and learner in which are developed the capacities, skills, understandings and modes of appreciation through which the learner comes to see the world in a more valuable way. Such value lies in, for example, the improved capacity to control the physical environment or to understand the social and economic forces. But such particular learning activities are to be seen within a broader 'educational practice' in which are embodied aims and values. Teachers do not act on their own. They are part of a larger enterprise, and their authority derives from their participation in that enterprise. They are the mediators of a culture to the growing minds of the learner. The classroom is not a platform for promoting the private views, but a forum in which the public understandings and procedures we have inherited are communicated to another generation. And, therefore, educational discourse (that is, the way in which we talk about educational practice) must embrace this broader moral purpose in which the development of persons is central. It must respect the complex way in which learning is achieved. *A fortiori*, that discourse must respect the way teaching is an essential part of that learning achievement through its introduction to a public world of knowledge, criticism and values.

EDUCATIONAL DISCOURSE

How we see the world depends upon the concepts through which experience is organized, objects identified as significant, descriptions applied and evaluations made. I have argued that talk about education should not evade the essentially moral concepts and language indispensable to the description of persons and their development. *A fortiori*, research into education must refer to the world so described and evaluated. Otherwise, it is research into something else. Beware, therefore, those who, in the interests of research or political control, try to change the language of education.

The danger might be illustrated as follows. A top civil servant, in giving an account of the nature and purposes of policy changes, said that we must 'think in business terms'. That meant that we look at those changes, as engineered by government, as a 'quality circle' in which one defines the product, defines the process, empowers the deliverer, measures the quality, empowers the client, and develops partnership. The 'product' is defined in terms of a detailed, outcomes-related National Curriculum. The 'process' is spelt out in terms of the proven 'effectiveness' route into the production of this 'product'. The changed management structures 'empower the deliverers' of the 'process' to satisfy the needs of the respective 'stakeholders'. The measurement of the quality of the 'product' is provided through a detailed National Assessment or a 'testing against product specification'. The 'empowering of the clients' comes about through the creation of choice and through the availability of data on effectiveness and through competitiveness amongst the 'deliverers of the product' so that the clients can exercise choice. And 'developing partnerships' are created for 'stakeholders', 'deliverers' and 'clients' to work together in developing the 'effective processes' for producing the 'product' (which, incidentally, has been defined by someone external to the 'process'). The management of the whole process is conducted by what Mark Freedland refers to as 'imposed contractualism' – the cascading down from above of production targets (in Faulkner *et al.*, 1999).

My argument was, and is, that the language of education through which we are asked to 'think in business terms' constitutes a new way of thinking about the relation of teacher and learner. It employs different metaphors, different ways of describing and evaluating educational activities. In so doing, it changes those activities into something else. It transforms the moral context in which education takes place and is judged successful or otherwise. Researchers of educational practice cannot ignore the language through which that practice is described and evaluated.

The effect of this new language is not a matter for empirical enquiry alone, for that which is to be enquired into has become a different thing. So mesmerized have we become with the importance of 'cost efficiency' and 'effectiveness' that we have failed to see that the very nature of the enterprise to be researched into has been redefined. Once the teacher 'delivers' someone else's curriculum with its precisely defined 'product', there is little room for that *transaction* in which the teacher, rooted in a particular cultural tradition, responds to the needs of the learner. When the learner becomes a 'client' or 'customer', there is no room for the traditional apprenticeship into the community of learners. When the 'product' is the measurable 'targets' on which 'performance' is 'audited', then little significance is attached to the 'struggle to make sense' or the deviant and creative response.

Indeed, the metaphors taken from management do not embody values other than those of efficiency and effectiveness. It is as though (within the discourse of management) there are two quite different sorts of conversation: that which concerns the efficient means to the attainment of clearly defined goals, and that which concerns the goals towards which we should seek to be efficient. The result is a language of 'ends' and objectives established outside the process of being educated – the endless lists of competencies, the 'can dos' which might be objectively measured. 'Education', then, becomes the means to achieve these ends, and it is judged essentially by its effectiveness. If it is not effective, then it should adopt other 'means', based on the kind of research which relates means to ends – that is, what the teacher does to what the learner can do as a result. 'Means' are logically 'separated' from the 'ends', and the quality of the 'input' is measured simply by reference to the success or otherwise of the 'output'.

The mistake is twofold. First, such a list of competencies cannot do justice to the quality and depth of thinking associated with the 'educated person', namely, the serious engagement with ideas, the struggle to make sense, the entry into a tradition of thinking and criticism, the search for value in what is often mundane, the excitement in intellectual and aesthetic discovery. Second, the 'ends' cannot be disconnected from the 'means' of achieving them. The engagement between teacher and learner as they endeavour to appreciate a poem or to understand a theorem or to solve a design problem is both the means and the end. For, as Dewey argued, the so-called 'end' becomes the 'means' to yet further thinking – the pursuit of yet further goals. But that is probably why Dewey for so long has been on the index of forbidden books in teacher training – a different language from that of management and control.

RESEARCHING 'EDUCATIONAL PRACTICE'

Many different sorts of study do in fact come under the heading of educational research. A large university department will conduct research into comparative education, the history of education, educational administration and so on. Many such researchers feel no need to enter schools or be interested in how and what children learn. They would no doubt be as happy outside the education department – in, say, departments of psychology or sociology. But the distinctive focus of educational research must be upon the quality of learning and thereby of teaching. With few exceptions, the classroom, and the transaction between teacher and learner in all its complexity, are what research should shed light upon. It is essentially eclectic and draws upon the theoretically more funda-mental work of sociologists and psychologists, but is not the same as it nor can it be logically reduced to it.

However, no such transactions can be considered in isolation from others, that is, from a programme of activities that together constitute an 'educational practice'. By a 'practice' I mean a collection of different activities that are united in some common purpose, embody certain values and make each of the component activities intelligible. For example, the teaching of a particular concept in mathematics can be understood only within a broader picture of what it means to think mathematically, and its significance and value can be understood only within the wider evaluation of the mathematics programme. What makes this particular activity intelligible is this broader picture of a range of interconnected activities, together with the value attributed to them.

It is impossible to overemphasize this point. In observing a classroom, I see a particular activity taking place – let us say, the teaching of the medieval field system to a group of 15 year olds. But such an activity makes *educational* sense only within a broader framework. Such a framework would contain or refer to the interlocking concepts within which the medieval field system makes sense or gains significance – the mode of ploughing, the rotating of crops, the obligation of peasant to landlord, etc. Such a framework, too, would have implicitly built into it the value of learning these concepts and of teaching them in this way. No *one* activity makes sense in itself. It is engaged within a broader spectrum of activities that have a unifying purpose. Such activities embody (perhaps inadequately or unreflectively) a set of under-standings about what is worthwhile learning, how learning should be pursued, what authorities should be respected.

By 'practice', therefore (following the lead of Carr, 1995), I mean the range of activities which cannot be seen in isolation but which are intelligible from an educational point of view because they encapsulate not only what should be learnt but also *how* that which is learnt should be transmitted. To probe beneath the activities – to make explicit that which makes them intelligible – is to reveal the nature of the 'educational practice'. Two sets of activities might, on the surface, appear to be very similar; one might be tempted to say they are the same educational practice. But further probing, revealing different explanations, purposes and values, might suggest the very opposite. Moreover, what appears to be effective within an educational practice, defined in one way, might prove to be ineffective when it is defined in another. Thus, rote learning of historical dates might seem highly effective within an educational practice where the capacity to repeat such dates is seen as part of a broader worthwhile activity, but highly ineffective when the purpose of learning history includes a care for and a love of the subject.

An educational practice, therefore, is a transaction between a teacher and a learner within a framework of agreed purposes and underlying procedural values. Such a transaction respects the learning needs of the learner, on the one hand, and, on the other, mediates the aspects of the culture which meet those needs. Such aspects include a tradition of literature and literary criticism, the narratives picked out by history, the understandings of the physical world embodied within the different sciences, the appreciation of the social worlds reflected in the arts. And, of course, such traditions, narratives, understandings and appreciations are by no means static. They are the product of deliberations, arguments, criticisms within and 'between the generations of mankind'. Therefore, the transaction between teacher and learner, at its best, might be seen as an initiation into what Oakeshott (1972) refers to as that conversation between the generations, in which the learner comes to understand and appreciate the voices of history, science, literature, etc. Many teachers – of English, say, or of science – see themselves as participating in such a tradition. They speak from a love of their subject and wish to convey that. They believe that the understanding enshrined within that tradition, of which they are the custodians, is important to the young people as they seek a deeper appreciation and knowledge of their lives and of the challenges within them. The teachers want, as it were, to bring the young people on the 'inside' of those traditions. Hence, it would be wrong to characterize such teaching activities by reference to some further 'end' or 'goal' logically disconnected from the activity of teaching. The goal, aim, value, purpose is embodied within the practice. One might refer to it as an element within a particular form of life, a way of thinking, a mode of valuing, into which the learner is being invited or even seduced.

Such a way of seeing an educational activity is to be contrasted with one in which an activity is geared simply to the production of something else – something only contingently or even arbitrarily connected with the activity itself. This latter distinction between 'means' and 'ends' tends to dominate a particular research tradition within the social sciences. In such a tradition, the targeted outcomes are 'given' – and defined as clearly and as measurably as possible. What is demanded of research is the evidence (based on experiment, if possible) that certain activities or interventions will ensure those outcomes.

CONCLUSION: THE EDUCATED COMMUNITY AND A LEARNING SOCIETY

Because of the criticism of educational research referred to in chapter 1, much educational research is dismissed as of poor quality. Therefore, what is funded may need to fit within the research framework of those who fund research (mainly government). But several problems arise:

First, the research questions asked may not be the proper ones to ask, having little to do with 'educational practice'. We need to remind ourselves of the complexity of the concept of education, in particular the evaluative nature of it and the different ways in which its focus, namely, the promotion of learning, is affected by the logically different ways in which learning is structured. Beware of general theories!

Second, the research method favoured, for that very reason,

might derive mainly and inappropriately from the social sciences. There is a danger, under pressure to produce clear, research-based guidance, to look uncritically to the social sciences for the right model of research. I say 'uncritically', not because the social sciences have nothing to offer, but because the *practice* of education cannot be the object of a science.

Third, the language of the research, reflecting the interests and requirements of those who manage the system, often gives an impoverished account of that which is to be researched into. There is a need to attend, at one level, much more rigorously than is often the case to the concepts and ideas employed (language too often is allowed to run away with itself) and, at another level, to the philosophical problems raised by inappropriate language.

Going back to Chicago, with which we started this chapter, what sense can be made of educational research and theorizing unless it attempts to make sense of the practice of educating and unless it addresses the problems as they are perceived by those who are engaged in it? And what status can such research have unless it contributes to a growing public understanding of situations, howsoever provisional and subject to further growth through criticism, upon which teachers, as learners, can draw in their 'problem-solving' and to which they might contribute in the light of experience and criticism? The interconnection between practising and theorizing is such that to institutionalize their separation is to make the theory irrelevant to the practice and the practice impervious to theoretical considerations. Perhaps this is the lesson to be learnt from Chicago.

Different kinds of research and their philosophical foundations

TWO TRADITIONS

Carr (1995) draws a distinction between two quite different and warring philosophical traditions which have dominated educational research. On the one hand, there is a tradition that sees educational research as a subset of the social sciences. Thus, it seeks the general laws or conditions which will enable teachers or policy-makers to predict what will happen if ... It seeks to establish empirically the most efficient and effective ways of attaining certain goals. The goals might be established by government (for example, that X% of 16 year olds achieve examination Grades A to C); these are the easily measured 'outcomes' to be pursued. Researchers would show what schools must do to reach those targets – how they might be effective.

Therefore, educational research has been dominated by empirical enquiries, initially from within educational psychology, but more recently from within sociology. 'Learning theory' was included in the training of teachers until comparatively recently. Such theory or theories included, for example, reference to the 'instinct theory' of McDougal who defined psychology as 'the positive science of the conduct of living creatures', and to Hull's *Principles of Behaviour*. The behaviourist traditions of Pavlov, Watson, Thorndike and Skinner were evolved to produce effective ways of managing classrooms through behaviour modification or through the establishment of principles of reinforcement and reward (see Peters, 1974, chapters 1 and 2).

Although such theories now seem to be largely neglected, the scientific model is not. Indeed, as Carr points out, it is assumed to be the most appropriate one in the introductions to textbooks on educational research. Cohen and Mannion's popular text quotes

Kerlinger's definition of research as 'the systematic, controlled, empirical and critical investigation of hypothetical propositions about the presumed relationships among natural phenomena' (Cohen and Mannion, 1985, p. 5). Indeed, educational progress is seen to have been 'slow and unsure' because of this failure to be truly scientific, relying upon unreflective experience, common sense, 'subjective' views, untested opinion.

Such views are assumed in not a little of the research into effective schools. They influence, too, the advocacy of evidence-based educational policy and practice where the model of randomized controlled tests in medicine is being translated into other public services including education (see Davies, 1999 and Petrosino *et al.*, 1999).

However, in the previous chapter's account of educational practice, I referred to that nurturing of the mental capacities through which the learners come to know, understand, judge, reflect and behave intelligently. There is something logically distinctive about such mental descriptions, indicating the inappropriateness of the scientific model. A proper description of an *educational* activity – that transaction between teacher and learner through which the learner comes to see and to understand in a different, more definitive manner – cannot avoid reference to the 'mental state' (the perceptions, understandings, feelings, and indeed valuings) of the learner. And, in a sense, these have a 'life of their own'. Present thoughts shape future reactions; future understandings to some degree are adaptations or reconstructions of previous ones. Therefore, it is concluded that the scientific model is simply not appropriate. There is a world of difference between the sort of enquiry appropriate for understanding physical reality and the sort of enquiry for understanding the mental life of individual persons. 'Man' is not 'a subject of science'.

For that reason, a quite different tradition of educational research has prevailed – one which purports to reveal the understandings and perceptions of the subjects of research – 'the phenomenology' of the mind. Such are the peculiarities of each person's perceptions and interpretations of events that significant generalization is impossible. Persons cannot be the object of scientific enquiry (though no doubt their biological functioning can be). Since an 'educational practice' is where individuals 'make sense' (starting from their different perspectives) of experience, struggle to understand, and come to find value in different things and activities, then it cannot be grasped within general laws or theories. Educational enquiry becomes focused upon individuals, making explicit what is unique and distinctive of the 'thinking life' of each, and interpreting what is seen through the personal ideas which make each action intelligible.

Such a clear dichotomy between different research traditions (what Dewey (1916), p. 323, would refer to as 'false dualisms') permeates so much of research writing. It is reflected in the contrast between the objective world of physical things and the subjective world of 'meanings', between the public world of outer reality and the private world of inner thoughts, between the quantitative methods based on a scientific model and the qualitative methods based on a kind of phenomenological exposure.

One main purpose of this book is to show that such dichotomies are mistaken, that researchers have fallen into a philosophical trap, which is very old indeed. It is the ancient dualism between mind and body, between the publicly accessible and the privately privileged. Educational research is both and neither. This I need to explain in detail.

THE VARIETY OF EDUCATIONAL RESEARCH

One notable feature of educational research is the variety of it. Different approaches are used to answer different questions. That, of course, makes sense where that which is being researched into, namely, educational practice, is a complex phenomenon. Different sorts of question require different sorts of research. Researchers must be eclectic in their search for the truth.

But behind these different approaches may also lie more fundamental differences of a philosophical kind. And, indeed, disagreement between researchers is as often as much a disagreement over the assumptions behind a research method as it is one over the most effective way of proceeding. This I want to illustrate by reference to a range of approaches which one might think of adopting.

Observing what happens

It may seem common sense that, if one wants to know something, one goes out and has a look. To know what works requires careful observation, the systematic recording of those observations and the attempt to generalize from them. The more observations there are which support the generalization, the more confident one might be in the conclusions reached. Thus, theory is gradually built up inductively from what is systematically recorded. Such a theory, when confirmed again and again, can then be used to predict observable outcomes and to guide practice. One can imagine such observation-based theory on such matters as how to maintain control of a class, how to teach irregular verbs, or how to create the 'effective school'.

The key feature in undertaking such observations would be consistency of approach. There is an awful amount to observe, and there is the danger that different observers might be looking for different things, or that the same observer might change the viewpoint from which he or she observes, thereby not allowing general conclusions to be drawn. For that reason, there were created 'observation schedules', the most famous of which was that by Flanders (see Flanders, 1970). Such a schedule divided the lesson into timed sections, and there were clear instructions to observe only certain things and to record behaviours for each of those sections. Thus, one would be able to observe accurately the exact amount of teacher talk as opposed to student talk or silences. Moreover, the schedule could be used by other observers, and, with the same instructions, they would be able to arrive at the same conclusions. Or, using the same schedule, they would be able to observe other lessons and, on the basis of records, make useful comparisons. These observations, when extended to enough cases, would enable the researcher to make generalizations which could be tested out against further observations, obtained and recorded in exactly the same way. Thus, a theoretical position could be built up.

It was thus the hope that there could be developed a science of teaching or of curriculum practice, just as there had been a science (constructed through careful observation, generalization and verification) of the physical world. What was wanted was an agreed base for making the observations and a painstaking effort to gather and to check the evidence. And the spirit of this aspiration is caught in the observation of one researcher who claimed that in any one lesson a thousand interactions take place between teacher and learner. It is as though an 'interaction' is some thing which can be isolated, observed and added to all the other interactions.

There are many examples of influential research which emphasize observation conceived in this way. The research into 'behaviour modification' required the careful defining of that which was to be observed in precise, behavioural and thereby observable terms (see Gurney, 1980). The researchers felt able therefore to correlate certain behaviours with certain conditions and to test out, through systematic observation, what happened once those conditions were changed. Or, again, examination output can be seen as a kind of observable behaviour which, in pursuit of the generalizations about 'effective schools', is to be correlated with observations about how those schools are managed or how the teachers behave. Thus, inspectors circulate with observation schedules, and teachers receive numerical scores on the basis of what is observed.

In one sense, of course, observation is necessary. But that necessity should not be allowed to obscure certain things. First, observations do not come independent of concepts and theories, apart from the prejudices and preferences we bring to the observing. Take for example the request to observe the different objects in the room. Very soon one finds oneself in the logical difficulty of deciding what is an object for this purpose. Are these several people or one family? Is this one object (a chair) or five objects (four chair legs and a seat)? Is that picture on the wall one thing (a picture) or several things (the painting, the frame and the cord with which to hang it or them)? Second, as I shall show, it is not clear that it is the *behaviour* that I am observing. For example, two teachers who appear to be doing the same thing, may in fact be doing two very different things – as when both seem to be teaching but one is mimicking the other. Two pupils write the same answer in the same circumstances, but one has worked it out through a complex formula, the other has guessed or relied on memory. What appear on the surface to be the same behaviour are in fact two very different ones, but this we know only by reference to the intentions and mental activities of those who are being observed.

Therefore, we are beginning to see certain difficulties in too much dependence on observation as such. First, observations are 'filtered', as it were, through the understandings, preferences and beliefs of the observer. Second, what is observed is not open to immediate acquaintance – the meanings and motives of those who are observed need to be taken into account.

I shall return to this point in chapter 4 (see 'Key Concepts') and chapter 5 (see 'Interpretive Theory'). But one can, no doubt, already see how far-reaching are the philosophical issues. Is this the *real* world that I am observing – or one that is interpreted through my own personal (and subjective?) scheme of things? What is the connection between the language through which I choose to describe the world and the world itself, existing independently of me? And does the *human* world, which I want to describe, actually exist independently of me, that is, of my interactions with it and of my interpretations of it? We take for granted that our 'common sense' account of the world is accurate enough. But it may be the case that such a world is as distorted in its conception of things as was the pre-Copernican world which was convinced from experience that the sun went round the earth.

Experimenting
One aspect of the scientific paradigm, which educational research might emulate, is the experimental design in which there is a control and an experimental group. One might say that the experimental approach is a more systematic approach to observation, as one carefully adjusts different elements and carefully observes, in a very controlled way, the results of the adjustment.

Such control and experimental groups need to be carefully selected and sufficiently large for conclusions to be drawn about the larger population. For this to happen it is seen to be desirable for the groups to be selected on a randomized basis; one compares the performance of the two groups in the light of a specific intervention in the experimental group. Research based on randomized controlled groups is, of course, well established in medical sciences. Thus, if one wants to know the impact of a particular drug, then one randomly selects two groups of patients, and then, keeping all other variables constant, observes carefully the effect on one group of the use of this particular drug. The groups have to be large to play down the significance of 'rogue factors' or particular exceptions to the general case.

There are many examples of such research in the area of education, and one can see the temptation to extend the approach more widely. For example, Sylva and Hurry's (1995) research into intervention in reading difficulties compares two different interventions with a control group. Therefore, it might be concluded that, if one group scores significantly more highly on reading scores after the period of intervention, then the intervention itself was a significant factor. It might even be said that the intervention itself was the *cause* of the difference.

The concept of 'cause' is one we shall need to examine more closely in chapter 4. But we seem now to be shifting into the very scientific paradigm which has been questioned. Is there not a danger of ignoring those individual differences, reflected in their own distinctive consciousness, in order to treat each of the several thousand children as identical units to be added together, subtracted and compared? How can this approach to research be reconciled with the apparent uniqueness of each individual? On the other hand, the uniqueness of each individual in certain respects does not entail uniqueness in every respect. There would seem to be certain aspects of being human which at least enables us to make tentative generalizations about how individuals will perform or react – whilst at the same time recognizing that there will inevitably be exceptions to the rule. Does the recognition of the distinctively personal mode of consciousness preclude any commonality and therefore generalization (howsoever tentative) about human motive, aspiration, valuing, mode of learning, etc.?

Such puzzles make one query the rather rigid separation of the quantitative from the qualitative approaches to research – and the clear distinction often made between the objective, observable and measurable world of science, on the one hand, and, on the other, the subjective and non-measurable world of individual consciousness. Perhaps we exaggerate the uniqueness of each person. Perhaps we make too sharp a break between the 'private' and 'subjective' consciousness and the 'public' and 'objective' world, both physical and social. Given human nature being what it is and given the physical conditions necessary for mental operations, then maybe generalizations are possible, verified by observations howsoever guarded these may be. This subtle interconnection between the public and the private, the objective and the subjective, the physical and the mental, the personal and the social, is too often neglected by those who espouse 'research paradigms' which embrace one side of the dichotomy to the exclusion of the other.

Surveying what is the case

One way of evading some of these difficulties would seem to be the *survey*. This calls upon the views of those who matter, but does so in a way that can lead to generalization.

The survey does not depend upon an outside observer who, recording what is observable, fails to take into account the views of those who are observed – which views might affect the conclusions drawn. The ideas, and not just the observable behaviours, of the teachers or learners might be wanted. Putting together a survey would seem to be the obvious way forward. That is, one simply asks people through a questionnaire.

Moreover, when, for example, a researcher wants to know a great deal from several schools, then observation would not seem to be practically possible. One could, of course, employ an enormous number of observers. But, first, this would be expensive; second, there would be problems over reliability between so many observers. In any case, it might not be a matter of observation alone.

The survey, however, does not escape completely the problems raised by straightforward observation. Very often it seeks to build up the evidence which can then be quantified – X% say this, Y% say that, and so on. There are sophisticated ways of getting this information and of checking the reliability of the answers. But there are limitations built into the approach. Thus, just as the researchers bring their own distinctive ways of looking at the world to their observations, so do those being researched bring their own understandings to answering the questions. Two parents might both answer 'yes' to the question 'Is your child's school a successful one?', but mean different things by that – one associating success with achievements against national norms in public examinations, the other interpreting success in terms of prowess at sport. Or, even if they both agree with what is meant, they may be ignorant in different ways of the implications of what they agree to. If they knew the implications, they might have given different answers. There *can be* something logically odd, therefore, in simply adding together the different answers to questionnaires and surveys and giving a score. It is as though all the answers added together are all of the same logical kind. But, if the same mark on the paper represents different understandings, then they should not be added up as though they mean the same thing.

There is, therefore, a tendency in much criticism of such research to reject it out of hand. It is seen to 'reify' (that is, make it into a 'thing', existing independently of my or others' thinking about it) that which is significant only in relation to the thoughts, feelings, intentions of the people concerned. It quantifies that which is not open to adding and subtracting and multiplying. It is, in other words, an extension of the 'scientific/mathematical' paradigm which is inappropriate to an understanding of human beings.

One must be careful, however, in pursuing this line too far. In saying this, I am indicating my general criticism of so much discourse on educational research, which, not attending to the deeper philosophical issues, polarizes the debate between the scientific paradigm and the humanistic, between the quantitative methodology and the qualitative. Thus, there are many questions which are fairly unambiguous to fluent users of the English language. The meanings which the respondents attribute to the questions are not something private and subjective, but the meanings which anyone conversant with the language would attribute to them. Therefore, where one can be sure that there is no ambiguity in the questions or where personal beliefs are unlikely to change the significance of the questions, it makes sense to tot up how many people agree with this or disagree with that. But such uses must be limited, because so many questions do raise issues on which there is disagreement over interpretation as well as over the facts. It is always reasonable to ask further what a person meant by answering the question in the way that he or she did.

Interviewing

The answer to the problems, referred to above, connected with the systematic observation of behaviours, or with the wide-scale surveys of what people do or believe, would seem to lie in letting the 'objects' of research – for example, the teachers or the students – speak for themselves. What significance do *they* attach to the action observed or the activity pursued? Typically the researcher, in seeking answers to certain questions, will structure the interview so that the answers will be relevant to the researcher's interests. But the interview will normally be only semi-structured because otherwise there would not be the scope for those interviewed to expound the full significance of their actions. If you believe that the significance or the 'meaning' of what is done lies in the ideas, intentions, values and beliefs of the agent, then those ideas, etc. have to be taken into account. The good interviewer is able to draw out from the person interviewed the deeper significance of the event, so much so that it seems ever more difficult to generalize – to see this or that individual as simply an instance of a generalization. The individual's consciousness and intentions are the significant factors in explaining why things happen as they do.

This seems very plausible, and the result has been the growth of studies which seek an understanding of particular events through the eyes of the participants. But there are difficulties.

First, of a practical kind, such studies can be of interest only to those who are in that unique situation – unique because to be understood only through the ideas and beliefs of the 'actors' within the situation. But quite clearly those who seek to improve educational practice or those who are responsible for developing educational policy want more than a collection of studies which, however interesting in themselves, have nothing to say beyond the particular events and contexts studied. Hence, the quite justified criticism that educational research is often too small-scale and fragmented to serve policy and professional interests.

Second, however, what lies behind this apparently practical difficulty and criticism is a difficulty of a more philosophical kind. Given the claimed uniqueness of each individual's understanding of an event or an activity, it would seem impossible for the interviewer to grasp the significance of what is said. The interviewer inhabits his or her own unique world of beliefs and understandings. The responses would need to be filtered through those, and thereby become different from the beliefs and understandings of the person interviewed. This difficulty and the answer to it are developed later. All sorts of device are invoked by those researchers who want to preserve the uniqueness and essential subjectivity of the private worlds of the people researched into. For example, meanings are 'negotiated' between researcher and researched, as indeed they are claimed to be between any persons engaged in conversation. But such metaphors do not really get us out of the hole already dug between the objective world espoused by those within the 'scientific paradigm' and the subjective world of intentions, beliefs and meanings espoused by those who reject such a paradigm.

Let us leave it there for the moment. We have seen the importance attached to a particular way of engaging in research (the semi-structured interview) which meets some of the criticisms, partly philosophical, arising from reliance upon observation, survey and experiment. But, unless one is careful, this antidote is equally problematic. This is because, in my view, which will be argued at greater length later, a dichotomy between the public and the private, between the objective and the subjective, has been created which cannot be justified.

Case studying
This emphasis upon the uniqueness of events or actions, arising from their being shaped by the meanings of those who are the participants in the situation, points to the importance of the 'case study' – the study of the unique case or the particular instant. This is reflected in the rather paradoxical title of Helen Simons's edited book on case study, *Towards a Science of the Singular* (Simons, 1981). Such a study would start from the premise that any unit of investigation in which persons were involved could only be understood if the perspectives of those involved (and the interaction of those perspectives) were taken into account. Indeed,

these would be central to the research. But, of course, that would make what was being researched unique and not open to generalization.

The 'unit' studied might be a person, an institution or a collection of institutions (such as a local education authority). Obviously, the larger the unit the more complex becomes the unravelling of the interactions and the perspectives. None the less, the claim would be made that, without such in-depth detective work, one would not really understand what was going on. Examples of thoroughgoing 'studies of the singular' in education would be Peshkin's (1978) *Growing Up American* and Hargreaves's (1967) *Social Relations in a Secondary School*.

These studies reveal a variety of methods – observations, surveys, interviews, etc. It is difficult to generalize. What they tend to have in common (although there are exceptions) is the following. First, there is an intensity in the examination of the particular. Second, it is believed that the unit under investigation cannot be understood except within the broader context of the understandings shared and not shared by the participants. Third, there is a disinclination to import an alien and theoretical language not used by the participants. Fourth, there is a responsiveness to the experience of 'the case'. Fifth, the distance between researcher and researched is narrowed such that the resulting study is more a 'negotiation' than a discovery of what is the case.

Thus, the case studies, despite the differences amongst them, tend to make assumptions which raise philosophical questions.

First, it is often assumed that the researcher, in coming to the investigation with an open mind, lets the data 'speak for themselves'. Hence, the popularity of Glaser and Strauss's (1967) 'grounded theory' – only gradually, in trying to make sense of one's experience, does one develop a theoretical position, and that 'emerging theory' is constantly tested out against further experience, data and questionings. Furthermore, that theoretical position remains close to the concepts and language shared with those being researched into. There is no privileging of a theoretical position imported from outside through which the data are looked for or selected.

Second, from such an intense study of the particular, it is not possible to generalize to other situations, although the graphic descriptions may alert one to similar possibilities in other situations. They, as it were, 'ring bells'. But general links between particular events or conditions and subsequent happenings cannot be established. That simply would not make sense.

Third, questions emerge about the *objectivity* of the research, the *reality* which is exposed and the *truth* of the claims being made. Indeed, these concepts, as we shall see in the following chapter, are interlinked. The objectivity is challenged precisely because the researchers cannot stand aside as though their presence had no effect upon the situation. Furthermore, the situation has to be described in a language which is employed by those who are being researched into. Otherwise, so the argument goes, it would not be *their* situation which is being investigated. The reality being researched has to be the reality as defined by the participants. Thus, there is talk of 'multiple realities', reflecting the different definitions of reality by the people involved in the research – that is, the 'realities' of different individuals whose 'definitions' of the situation are necessarily different from each other's. 'Objectivity' in the sense of getting at what exists 'out there', independently of researcher and researched, makes no sense.

The interrelated concepts of 'objectivity', reality' and 'truth' require careful consideration which I shall give in chapter 4. Indeed, how one makes sense of these concepts or employs them in educational research affects profoundly the significance attached to that research. A particular interpretation of them arises in some accounts of case study. I believe that many of these accounts are philosophically mistaken. However, despite this, I still insist upon the insights which case study, the study of the singular, brings – the study of the distinctive features of a particular situation without which that situation cannot be fully understood. (On the other hand, there is something peculiar in the phrase 'fully understood'. Events are understood for different purposes, and the degree of understanding required depends on those purposes.)

But the value of the 'study of the singular' should not blind us to those features of the study which limit the singularity. All situations are unique in some aspects, not in others. There is something distinctive about each individual, and yet something in common between this individual and that. The language through which we describe the singularity of one situation is the same language through which we describe the singularity of another. Concepts are necessarily general in their application. And so we must be careful, in studying the 'singular', not to draw quite mistaken philosophical conclusions about the inability to generalize.

Historical research

McCulloch and Richardson (2000), in their book *Historical Research in Educational Settings*, point to the dearth of literature on the application of historical research to the field of education – or, if you like, on the *reflection upon* doing history in education – even though there is so much written on the history of education. But it is important, where historical research is pursued, to explore what it means to think historically – not simply the distinctive skills which need to be acquired (let us say, in searching for and in interpreting documentary evidence), but also the competing philosophical traditions of what constitutes 'doing history' or 'thinking historically'. For example, there is the inevitable problem of understanding the text within the belief system of the time – the attempt to enter imaginatively into the mindset of people and institutions in a very different era and situation. The notion of 'historical imagination', or what the philosopher of history, R. G. Collingwood, referred to as 're-enactment', would seem to be crucial – but constantly open to revision when tested out against further evidence. But, more significantly for my purposes, is the centrality of historical understanding to a valid appreciation of the present, a realization that how we see ourselves, others and the world around us is itself (in part) a historical product, which can therefore be fully grasped only within a historical narrative. The way in which we conceptualize experience is not (and never has been) fixed for all eternity, but has a history, or has its roots in particular economic and social circumstances and to some extent has evolved through critical reflection and discussion.

But Collingwood's ideas of history (see Collingwood, 1946, but also Hughes-Warrington's (1996 and 1997) excellent accounts of Collingwood's historical/philosophical understanding of education) would not be universally accepted by philosophers of history. Historical research gets caught up in the ideological disputes which permeate the social sciences generally – Marxist, modernist and postmodernist.

There are, of course, other research approaches, which we should bear in mind, concerned with: studying other societies and groups (from their point of view); documentary enquiry; comparisons across cultures; action research. Some of these I shall be examining later in the book. But the ones above reveal the tendency to divide research into two different paradigms – the 'warring camps' to which Carr refers.

THE 'FALSE DUALISM' OF EDUCATIONAL RESEARCH: QUANTITATIVE AND QUALITATIVE

There is a danger in educational research, as indeed in everything, of drawing too sharp a contrast between different kinds of activity or different kinds of enquiry. And these sharp divisions are frequently 'institutionalized', with members of one 'institution' sniping at members of the other. Thus, in so many theses and books, a sharp distinction is made between quantitative and qualitative research. And the distinction is made on the basis not of 'appropriateness to task' but of 'epistemology' and even 'ontology'. Thus, the quantitative researchers are seen to have a distinctive view about the nature of our knowledge about the physical and the social world. And the qualitative researchers question that view, and very often reject the whole quantitative enterprise as 'epistemologically flawed'. Researchers work within different paradigms.

The differences are reflected in the respective languages of each and in the way in which key ideas or concepts take on a different logical character. By that I mean that these concepts, which seem unavoidable when we reflect philosophically upon the nature of enquiry, link together in logically different ways and take on slightly different meanings. Such words as 'objectivity' (and, by contrast, 'subjectivity'), 'reality' (and 'multiple realities'), 'truth' and 'verification', 'knowledge' and 'meaning' are interrelated and defined differently.

These concepts we shall look at more carefully in chapter 4. Here I wish to indicate how these differences in use and application frequently arise out of sharply contrasted ways of engaging in research. Thus Hodkinson (1998), in condemning Tooley's and Darby's report on educational research, refers to 'the deep ontological and epistemological problems that lie behind his essentially Cartesian approach'. It is not clear why Tooley was judged to be a follower of Descartes. Nor is it stated why, if that were the case, such a discipleship should be considered wrong. But evidently Tooley was understood to be resurrecting a clear distinction between the researcher and that which is researched, between a knowable world existing independently of the knower and the knower him or herself. By contrast, the qualitative researchers would seek to blur these distinctions. The world researched is affected by the research itself; our knowledge is a 'construction', reflecting the world, not as independent of our deliberations, but as something constructed by them.

In a nutshell, the contrast is drawn between quantitative research which is seen to be appropriate to the physical world (and wrongly applied to the personal and social) and qualitative research which addresses that which is distinctive of the personal and social, namely, the 'meanings' through which personal and social reality is understood. The latter simply cannot be quantified; it is not that sort of thing. Furthermore, the former kind of research is referred to as 'positivist', a word which has had a bad press amongst educational researchers and which therefore signals strong disapproval.

In chapter 5, I shall examine more closely what we mean by 'positivism'. It requires a more subtle and charitable understanding than many of its detractors afford it. But for my present purposes, it is enough to show how a clear distinction is made between explanations which generally pertain to the physical world, which are characterized by quantifiable generalizations, and which are frequently called positivist, and explanations which pertain to the non-physical world of personal and social meaning. The divide between the two sorts of explanation is seen to be 'epistemological'; that is, there are considered to be different underlying theories of explanation, of truth and of verification. And the divide is also seen to reflect 'ontological differences'; by that, I think, is meant that a particular philosophical position (namely, that the research gets at the world as it really is) applies to the first which does not to the second (namely, that the 'reality' researched can never be independent of the person researching it).

Here we see signs of the very Cartesian dualism which Hodkinson accuses Tooley of. And, indeed, it demonstrates the difficulty of avoiding such perennial dualism – namely, the clear distinction so often drawn between the physical and the mental, between body and soul, between the objective world (independent of our thinking about it) and the subjective world ('in our heads' and personally constructed), between 'things' and 'meanings'. And such Cartesian dualism is but one of the 'false dualisms' which Dewey (1916, chapter 25) criticizes. Dewey, of course, would never have denied there to have been a valid distinction between quantitative and qualitative – indeed, many more distinctions if we are to understand the complexity of the research questions and of the appropriate responses. But he would deny the 'epistemological' and 'ontological' apartheid which too often divides the qualitative and quantitative researchers. 'The world of real life' or 'the world of common sense' of which Ryle (1954), writes, cannot be captured by either the one or the other, and indeed there must be an integration and overlapping of the two.

It is important, therefore, to explore this divide a little further and to show how, in denying that which, at the everyday, common sense level, we find quite acceptable, is declared to be unacceptable by researchers. None the less, I want to add that the distinction, which is rightly drawn attention to, needs to be borne in mind lest research wrongly attempts to quantify that which cannot really be quantified.

The 'false dualism' which I have in mind is most effectively demonstrated in an influential book by Guba and Lincoln, *Fourth Generation Evaluation* (1989). The book sharply distinguishes between different generations of research – the first being the adoption of a quite inappropriate scientific model. By scientific the authors have in mind what would appear to many scientists as a rather impoverished model of science and one which would no doubt be characterized as 'positivist'. However, the poverty of the scientific model did, over time, become clearer, and so there was gradual progression to the fourth and superior paradigm which Guba and Lincoln espouse. The contrast between the first and the fourth paradigm is hinted at in this passage:

> Evaluation outcomes are not descriptions of the 'way things really are' or 'really work', or of some 'true' state of affairs, but instead represent meaningful constructions that individual actors or groups of actors form to 'make sense' of the situations in which they find themselves. The findings are not 'facts' in some ultimate sense but are, instead, literally *created* through an interactive process that *includes* the evaluator (so much for objectivity!) as well as the many stakeholders ... What emerges from this process is one or more *constructions* that *are* the realities of the case. (p. 8, their italics)

Thus, the 'evaluation outcomes' do not describe 'the way things really are' or 'really work'. Such is, as it were, the 'false ontology' of the first and scientific paradigm. It no longer makes sense to talk of the 'true' state of affairs. What, one might ask, is truth? Rather is it the case that we each, in our research and evaluations, try to 'make sense' of the situation we find ourselves in. We do this through 'constructing' connections, meanings, frameworks through which experience is sieved and made intelligible. 'Facts' are not discovered, but created.

These 'creations' and 'constructions' are clearly influenced by the values which the researchers bring to the situation – something unrecognized, apparently, by those working within the scientific paradigm. None the less, despite the influence of such personal constructions and reconstructions, people of like minds and like values may, through a process of 'negotiation', come to share the same values and reach a consensus over the way in which experience is to be understood – and thus about the validity of the research and its findings.

The 'fourth generation' of evaluation, therefore, argues that 'realities' are not objectively 'out there' but 'constructed' by people as they attempt 'to make sense' of their surrounds (which surrounds do not exist independently of them anyway). The new paradigm

> exists in what we have come to call the constructivist paradigm [which] rests on a relativist rather than a realist ontology, and on a monistic, subjective rather than a dualistic, objective epistemology. [This paradigm] is not, in sharp contrast to conventional methodology, a set of conclusions, recommendations, or value judgements, but rather an *agenda for negotiation* of those claims, concerns and issues that have not been resolved in the hermeneutic dialectic exchanges. (p. 13)

This view of research is to be contrasted with 'the first generation', the 'ontological' and 'epistemological' foundations of which are described in the following way:

> The methodology employed in evaluation has been almost exclusively scientific, grounded *ontologically* in the positivist assumption that there exists an objective reality driven by immutable natural laws, and *epistemologically* in the counterpart assumption of a duality between observer and observed that makes it possible for the observer to stand *outside* the arena of the observed (p. 12, their italics)

The contrast, philosophically, I have summarized in a recent paper in the *Journal of Philosophy of Education* (Pring, 2000) as follows:

First, the 'scientific paradigm' (paradigm A) believes in 'an objective reality'; the 'constructivist paradigm' (paradigm B), denying this, says that reality is a 'social construction of the mind', with as many constructions and thus realities as there are individuals. Thus, since science itself must be, on this thesis, a social construct, there are no immutable laws of cause and effect to be discovered.

Second, paradigm A believes in the separateness of researcher and researched; paradigm B blurs the distinction – the research 'findings' being created (not discovered) through the interaction between researcher and that which is researched.

Third, therefore, whereas paradigm A, in separating the researcher from the researched, has a notion of truth as correspondence between the research account and what is the case independently of the researcher, paradigm B's 'truth' is a matter of 'consensus' amongst informed and sophisticated constructors. 'Fact' does not exist independently of how the researcher constructs reality; it is not, as in paradigm A, that which makes true propositions true.

Finally, therefore, what is researched is to be understood only within the context with which, and through which, it has been constructed, thereby precluding generalizations. Neither problem nor its solution can be generalized from one setting to another.

There is a danger, as critics have pointed out, of setting up straw men to illustrate and to justify my accusation that researchers have created a 'false dualism' between the quantitative and the qualitative modes of research. There are many distinctions to be made within the qualitative tradition, each with its distinctive way of engaging in enquiry and of making intelligible the personal and social reality which is being portrayed. And, indeed, the scientific paradigm, too, could be seen as a caricature – as a view of science (narrow, impoverished, 'positivist') which by no means does justice to the distinctions and different perspectives marked out within the philosophy of science. The distinctions *within* the so-called paradigms are often as significant as the distinctions between them. Quantitative research will cover enquiries which range from the detailed measurement and correlation of performances within a strictly behaviourist tradition to the large-scale surveys of social trends within the tradition of 'political arithmetic'. Qualitative research embraces symbolic interactionism, phenomenology, ethnography, hermeneutics. And within any one piece of research there is often the employment of different approaches as different questions are addressed.

However, it is this failure to recognize the complexity of enquiry, and of the nature of that which is being enquired into, which causes the blurring of the distinctions within the so-called paradigms and results in the sharp dichotomy between them, characterized by contrasting conceptions of 'truth', 'reality' and 'objectivity'. The consequences for research are immense, with an inflated confidence in general explanations in the one case ('the causes of truancy', 'the science of teaching'), and with a total distrust of any general explanations in the other. One can see why those who look to research for guidance on the formulation of policy become disillusioned with an activity which denies the very possibility of providing it.

Let me look more carefully at the philosophical problems which so easily draw people into the rather simplistic and erroneous contrast between quantitative and qualitative modes of research.

The premises of those who are within paradigm A would seem to be as follows:

(a) There is a world which exists independently of me which is made up of 'objects' interacting causally with each other.
(b) There are different sciences of that world, partly depending on what is to count as an object (a 'behaviour', a 'physical object', even a 'social event').
(c) Once, however, there is an agreement on what is to count as an 'object' (e.g. behaviour), such objects can be studied, their interrelations noted, regularities discovered, causal explanations given and tested, results quantified.
(d) Other observers can check the conclusions through repeated experiments under similar conditions.
(e) Thus, from many carefully conducted observations and experiments, following critical checking from others, a scientifically based body of knowledge can be built up.
(f) That body of knowledge reflects the world as it is; the statements within it are true or false depending on their correspondence to the world as it is.

The premises of paradigm B are less easy to state, partly because truth lies not so much in correspondence between what we say and how things are, but in the 'consensus' which is 'negotiated'. But there is a paradox here. For the truth of this very position would itself be a matter of consensus. And those who share a different paradigm (let us say, paradigm A) might cheerfully state (using paradigm B's language) that they have socially constructed things differently – and happen to prefer the company of those who do believe there is a reality 'out there' and who do believe that an account of the world is either true or false (whether or not it can be verified for certain). Indeed, even Guba and Lincoln are obliged to have recourse to words and phrases which, more obscurely, imply much the same. Thus, 'through a hermeneutic dialectic process, a new construction will emerge that is not "better" or "truer" than its predecessors, but simply more informed and sophisticated than either' (p. 17). This takes place (note the extension of the metaphor of 'negotiation') in the 'academic marketplace of ideas'. Or, again, the hermeneutic/dialectic process 'creates a constructed reality that is as informed and sophisticated as it can be made at a particular point in time' (p. 44). Thus, not any kind of negotiation will do, only one which is informed (as opposed, presumably, to misinformed) and sophisticated (as opposed to naïve or lacking in subtlety).

It is difficult to state a philosophical position at this level of abstraction without falling victim to the implications of that position. Thus it was with the statement of the verificationist principle (see Ayer, 1946). But there is something peculiar about an argument for the abolition of 'truth' (as that is implied in paradigm B). This is implicitly recognized by Guba and Lincoln, though explicitly denied, in their recourse to such words as 'better informed', 'more sophisticated', 'more reasonable' and 'more appropriate'. In seeing the implications of this, one is forced to acknowledge 'reality' as something not entirely 'created' or 'constructed' or 'negotiated', but constraining and limiting – something which *is* independent of us, which shapes the standards of what we can *justifiably* say, and which restricts the conclusions that can be *correctly* drawn from the evidence given. And such 'realism' must permeate both quantitative and qualitative research.

None the less, in so arguing this, I am not thereby placing myself in paradigm A. Indeed, much that is labelled 'positivist' would not be 'realist' in the sense that I argue for (see, for example, Ayer, 1946). The difficulties which Guba and Lincoln create themselves arise from a dichotomy, a 'false dualism', an opposition established between the quantitative and the qualitative, which leads to anti-realism in both camps.

The premises of those within paradigm B seem to be as follows:

(a) Each person lives in a 'world of ideas', and it is through those ideas that the world (physical and social) is constructed. There is no way that one could step outside this world of ideas to check whether or not they accurately represent a world existing independently of the ideas themselves.

(b) Communication with other people, therefore, lies in a 'negotiation' of their respective worlds of ideas whereby, often for practical reasons (they need to live and work together), they come to share the same ideas. A consensus is reached.

(c) New situations arise and new people have to be accommodated with different ideas, so that negotiation within 'a marketplace of ideas' never ceases and new consensuses have constantly to be reached.

(d) Such notions as 'truth', therefore, need to be eliminated, or redefined in terms of 'consensus', because, given (a) above, there can be no correspondence between our conceptions of reality and that reality itself.

(e) Furthermore, the distinction between 'objective' and 'subjective' needs to be redefined since there can be nothing 'objective' in the sense of that which exists independently of the world of ideas which either privately or in consensus with others has been constructed.

(f) Development of our thinking (e.g. about educational problems and their solutions) lies in the constant negotiation of meanings between people who only partly share each other's ideas but who, either in order to get on practically or in order to accommodate new ideas, create new agreements – new ways of conceiving reality. Since there is no sense in talking of reality independently of our conceiving it, therefore there are as many realities as there are conceptions of it – multiple realities.

The 'false dualism' lies in the belief that, in rejecting paradigm A with its rather straightforward and uncomplicated 'correspondence theory of truth', researchers must inevitably embrace paradigm B. This, however, is simply not the case. It is possible to reject what is referred to as the 'positivism' of paradigm A without abandoning the realism of the physical and social sciences and without therefore concluding that reality is but a social construction or that correspondence between language and reality is to be thrown overboard completely.

Certainly, how we see the world does depend upon the ideas we have inherited. And, it is correct that different societies and social groups do, in important respects, conceive the world differently. Thus, we do in fact distinguish between different kinds of trees, but it is conceivable that we might not have done – distinguishing vegetation in terms of colour or shape or size. But the fact that we do so distinguish, although in a sense a social phenomenon, depends upon there being features of the world existing independently of me which makes such distinctions possible. The fact that there is an infinite number of ways in which we could divide up and classify things does not entail that any kind of distinction is possible. How we conceive things is embodied within a language and is inherited by those who learn that language. Far from individually constructing the world, we acquire those constructions which (although socially developed) are possible because of certain features of reality which make them possible. It is not that there are multiple realities. Rather are there different ways in which reality is conceived, and those differences may well reflect different practical interests and different traditions. Social constructionists in the sense of paradigm B are rarely found at 30,000 feet. Of course, not any social group has conceptualized the world in the same way as aeronautical engineers and scientists. But the possibility of so conceptualizing it is not itself a social construction – it is to do with certain conditions prevailing independently of our wishing them so. There are discoveries in mathematics (and those discoveries made air flight possible) as well as constructions.

That, it might be conceded, is true of the physical world – although that would be a big concession. One might, therefore, concede that there is a science of the physical world, but not one of the personal and social worlds. Our language of emotions, rights, intentions, attitudes, institutions would seem to be a social construction in a more thoroughgoing sense. Unlike the case of physical objects, there would seem to be no reality 'out there' independently of our creating it. Moreover, those creations are constantly reconstructed in the interactions between individuals. The moral words we use, the appraisals we make, the attributions of responsibility, the descriptions we give of motives and emotions have a history which, so it would seem, are located in particular social and cultural traditions, and evolve through the interaction between people within those traditions and between the traditions themselves. These constantly reconstructed ways of interpreting people and of relating to them, which have no reference outside the 'hermeneutic dialectic process' itself, cannot be true or false, objective or subjective as those terms are understood within paradigm A.

Again, however, the conclusions do not follow from the premises. Those premises are that the ways in which we describe, appraise or attribute responsibility within the personal and social sphere are themselves social constructs and that the 'reality' is somehow created and recreated through the very act of construction. Hence, what it *means* to be a person (for example, 'made to the image and likeness of God') is construed within particular groups and traditions. There is no *real* person independent of those constructions against which that account might be compared. There cannot, therefore, be a *true* account.

One needs, however, to attend to the intelligibility of making such a claim. The very possibility of the social interactions, through which social reality is construed, depends upon a shared understanding (howsoever vague and general) of what it is to be a person – a centre of consciousness capable of intentional action, rational behaviour, emotional response and potential for assuming some level of responsibility. It is true that the conceptual framework through which we think about 'persons' could have been different; the way, for example, in which we differentiate the emotions could have (as they no doubt do in other traditions) highlighted some features rather than others. There is no 'a priori' limit to the number of ways in which we might have conceptualized the social life. But that is not to say that there are *no* limits to how it might have been organized. The distinctions we make depend upon relatively stark features of human behaviour.

Just as the social construction of the physical world depends upon a real world, independent of that construction and constraining what construction is possible, so the social construction of the personal and social world presupposes the independent existence of objects (persons) which can be described in terms of consciousness, rationality, intentionality, responsibility and feeling. The very 'negotiation' of meanings can be conducted only within a framework of shared meanings, which meanings (in their most general state) are not open to negotiation. That is how the world is, independently of my construing it – and how it must be if I am to enter into negotiation with others.

Such a view reintroduces the unavoidable concepts of 'truth' and 'objectivity', albeit not in the sense of the naïve realism which is attributed to paradigm A. By 'naïve realism' I mean some sort of picture theory of truth in which the world as we conceive it is mirrored in the language through which we give an account of it. There is a one-to-one relation between the objects in the world and the nouns and pronouns which pick out those objects, between the nature of those objects and the descriptors within the language. It is the mistake of those who criticize paradigm A that they attribute such a correspondence theory of truth to any position other than that found in paradigm B. It is wrongly concluded that, since 'naïve realism' is unacceptable, one is obliged to adopt paradigm B in which the notion of 'reality' is dispensed with along with 'naïve realism'.

Bridges (1999) demonstrates the poverty of such a move. The concept of truth, as indeed the concept of reality, is both too complex and too indispensable to be so easily dismissed. My argument has been that, in the ways in which both physical and social realities are conceptualized, the very possibility of the negotiation of meanings presupposed the existence of things (including 'person things'). These things must have certain distinguishing features which make possible our different constructions of the world. It is always possible to refuse a construction imposed upon one, not from bloody-mindedness, not from lack of interest, but from the fact that such a construction is not possible – given that reality (physical and personal) is what it is.

Given that there are 'persons', objectively speaking, existing independently of my constructing them as persons, and given that there are 'societies' of 'persons', again existing in relatively stable conditions, then there seems to be no 'a priori' reason why such persons and societies cannot be studied as 'objects' and to some extent 'added up', 'multiplied', 'divided' and generalized about. And, indeed, it is that which policy-makers are often anxious to see as they deliberate about this policy to adopt or that intervention to sanction.

However, those who emphasize the distinction between quantitative and qualitative research are right in demanding caution in the extension of quantification to certain aspects of personal and social reality. How we describe that reality depends very much upon the purpose of the description. It may, for certain purposes, be sensible to talk of X number of people being angry at what happened or having understood the nature of the problem. But for other purposes, the nature of that anger or that understanding, reflecting the different ways in which the people conceived the situation, would be wrongly perceived as the same kind of thing in each case. Surveys which tot up similar responses to the same question might in fact give a very distorted picture of how the different people really felt about or understood a situation. And this becomes even more insidious where children's understandings, knowledge and attitudes are given numerical scores or grades, and these then compared with others' scores or grades, as though it is the 'same thing' being spoken about. For some strange reason, this problem is rarely acknowledged, and thus, under the urge to quantify, we reduce to an arithmetical unit the complexity of children's struggle 'to make sense' or to understand.

Behind the criticism of quantitative research lies an understandable suspicion of those who sponsor research and use its results in the interest of management. It is worth pointing out vigorously that educational arrangements are increasingly organized to serve economic and social interests as these are conceived by political leaders and that, in pursuing these ends, such leaders ask us to manage schools in the light of what research concludes to be the most 'effective' way of achieving them. It is equally true and worth pointing out that such research, in ignoring the complex transactions which take place between teacher and learner and which cannot be captured in the management, means/end language of that research, distorts those educational transactions, and 'disempowers' and 'disenfranchises' (Guba and Lincoln's words) the teachers. It is as though the 'managers', aloof from the education process, seek general solutions to generalized conceptions of the problem, and then, in the light of the evidence, tell the teachers what to do. The result lies in a failure to recognize the peculiarities and complexity of the specific context, the ways in which the situation must be understood from the perspective of the participant, and the denial of professional responsibility to the teacher.

The acceptance of paradigm B, in denying the intelligibility of such an understanding of research (the clear distinction between researcher and researched disappears in the 'negotiation' of meanings which takes place in the 'marketplace' of ideas), is seen to liberate the teacher from this management control. Each context is created through the 'hermeneutic dialectic process', as consensus is reached about an understanding of the situation. However, the shift to a paradigm where 'reality' (or the 'multiple realities') is (or are) totally created or constructed through the negotiation of meanings leaves the teacher vulnerable to a different sort of control. There are strong and weak negotiators, those practised in the art and skill, and those who are not. There is as much danger of the 'reconstructed realities' reflecting the dominance of those in powerful negotiating positions as there is of the researchers in paradigm A serving the interests of the educational managers. The links between knowledge, on the one hand, and power and control, on the other, are equally strong within both paradigms, albeit the nature of the connection is different. But this problem arises because of the severance of knowledge and understanding from some notion of reality independent of our construction of it. The one guarantee of freedom is that there are constraints on our construction of reality, namely, reality itself, and that it is always possible to challenge others' ideas and 'constructions' in the light of what is the case.

My argument is that the opposition (not the distinction) between quantitative and qualitative research is mistaken. The 'naïve realism' attributed to those who espouse the more quantitative methodology is not justified. How we conceive the world could be different and, indeed, is different from social group to social group. Such 'social constructions' are constantly reconstructed as new experiences force us to reshape how we understand things. Hence, the need for that interpretive and hermeneutic tradition in which we seek to understand the world from the perspective of the participants, or to understand a set of ideas from within the evolving tradition of which they are part. However, such differences in how we understand reality are possible because there are stable and enduring features of reality, independent of us, which make such distinctions possible. And this applies not simply to the physical world but also to the social and personal. There are features of what it is to be a person which enable generalizations to be made and 'quantities' to be added or subtracted. Most persons have predictable emotions and capacities which make it possible for certain purposes to consider them the same from person to person – and thus open to quantification. The qualitative investigation can clear the ground for the quantitative – and the quantitative be suggestive of differences to be explored in a more interpretive mode.

RESEARCH METHODS AND PHILOSOPHICAL ASSUMPTIONS

I started this chapter by referring to the way in which educational research seems to fall into two, philosophical and competing camps. One embraces a scientific model for understanding educational practice; the other emphasizes that human beings cannot be the objects of science and that research must focus upon the 'subjective meanings' of the learners.

However, attention to the many ways in which research is conducted reveals a more complicated picture. In some respects, people are the 'object of science' – of generalizations and causal explanations. In other respects, however, they escape such explanations through interpreting the world in their own personal ways. Yet again, such personal interpretations draw upon traditions, upon public ways of understanding the world, upon social customs and practices. Different methods get at these different explanations. Understanding human beings, and thus researching into what they do and how they behave, calls upon many different methods, each making complex assumptions about what it means to explain behaviours and personal and social activities.

The dominance of any one methodological approach to educational research gives priority (in some cases exclusive priority) to certain kinds of explanation, and thus to certain assumptions about human beings. Indeed, one could argue that some 'theory of human nature' lies behind any particular approach to educational research. By 'theory' I mean that cluster of beliefs and values which underpin our understanding of things and which become the premises upon which those explanations hang. However, other researchers might make very different presuppositions – and therefore adopt different methods.

The next two chapters aim to illustrate the philosophical presuppositions of these methodological differences.

—4

Key concepts and recurring conflicts in educational research

THE LOGICAL GEOGRAPHY OF EDUCATIONAL RESEARCH

The polarization between the two paradigms, which is typical of so much theoretical writing on educational research, bears little relation to the complexity of research practice or, indeed, to how we think about research at the intelligent common sense level. I shall postpone the account of what I mean by 'intelligent common sense' to the end of this chapter. It is a crucial antidote to much of the silliness which too many writers on educational research expose us to. But I want immediately to show how this polarization between the two paradigms causes us to interpret too narrowly and mistakenly key concepts and ideas in research – contrary to what we would assume if we were to attend to how these words were employed in practice.

Because of the importance of philosophy and the social sciences to an understanding of any social phenomenon or practice, educational research is necessarily caught up in the controversies which affect the nature and validity of the social sciences. These controversies reflect quite fundamental ways of conceptualizing our understanding of the world, especially the social world of people and institutions. These concepts or ideas provide the basic framework of intelligibility. And, therefore, the divisive controversies, which prevail in educational research, might best be approached through an examination of these key concepts. By referring to them as 'key concepts' I am pointing to their indispensability in our communication with other people and in our thinking about, and ordering of, our experience. Despite, however, their indispensability, the appropriate application is a matter of controversy, and where one positions oneself in these controversies affects one's views about the practice and the validity of research.

These key and fundamental concepts which we need to consider are:

(a) *'reality' and 'objectivity'*: what is the case independently of the researcher's personal or socially constructed ideas; and the procedures for understanding that reality;

(b) *'causal explanation'*: what it means to say that one has explained an event or a phenomenon by reference to another, usually antecedent, one;

(c) *'explanations of human behaviour'*: what constitutes a non-causal explanation of distinctively human behaviour;

(d) *'truth'*: what is being claimed when we say something is true or when we assume or assert the truth of an explanation;

(e) *'fact'*: what counts as fact as opposed to fiction or social construction, and the nature of the distinction made between 'fact' and 'value';

(f) *'theory'*: as opposed to common sense or practical under-standings; and the validity or truth of theoretical explanations;

(g) *'knowledge'*: what constitutes knowing (as opposed to merely 'believing' or 'having an opinion'), the growth of knowledge, and the links between 'knowledge', 'truth', 'certainty' and 'verification'.

Of course, it is artificial splitting key concepts up like this. Making sense of the one requires reference to the others. 'Explaining', for example, makes implicit reference to 'verification' and 'truth conditions'. Theories of truth have implications for what we mean by the 'objectivity' of statements and enquiries. There is a 'logical geography' in which these different concepts have their inter-connected places and provide an indispensable framework of intelligibility for research. And it is the aim of this chapter to map out these interconnections.

KEY CONCEPTS

Realism and objectivity
'Realism' is the view that there is a reality, a world, which exists independently of the researcher and which is to be discovered. Research is a matter of finding out about it. And the conclusions of the research are true or false, depending on whether they match up

to that reality. This at least would seem to be the common sense view.

But many, who theorize about research, would deny this to be the case. Confronted with difficulties about the meaning and nature of 'truth', and about the theory dependent understanding of reality, they have, like Guba and Lincoln (see chapter 3), denied there to be any such reality. Rather is reality 'socially constructed' and there are as many realities or 'multiple realities' as there are social constructions – which could be an enormous number. Research, therefore, is often focused upon people's 'perceptions of reality' where one lot of perceptions is as good as another. Their truth or falsity does not and cannot come into it.

If we distinguish between the physical and the social worlds, then this anti-realism gains some plausibility. The social, if not the physical, world would seem to be 'socially constructed'. Moreover, each person, in relationship to other persons and in negotiating with them the social reality which they might share, would be thought to *create* reality. Reality would not exist independently of individuals' personal creations against which they might assess or evaluate their perceptions.

It is interesting to note that the flip side of this position is the denial of any social reality at all – it has no existence other than what we choose to create. Hence, Mrs Thatcher would be correct in saying that there is no such thing as society, and (along with the politicians and advisors who followed and still follow her lead) in dismissing the kind of research which explains educational outcomes in terms of social facts.

The problem with this position, however, is that it fails to distinguish between the following. First, there are social forces and structures which we may not be conscious of but which none the less shape relationships; these are what social scientists seek to discover and to bring to our conscious understanding so that we can do something about them. Second, there are social understandings which we have inherited, which we are conscious of and which shape how we see the social world. Third, there are the processes through which we sometimes transform these understandings for our own purposes or as part of a much wider cultural change.

Let us take, for example, the 'social reality' of the family and the interconnected concepts of parent, sibling, extended relations including uncles, aunts, and so on. Connected with such interrelated concepts are others concerning rights and obligations (often legally embodied), loyalties and affections. These understandings, through which we understand what is happening independently of us, are not our creation, even though they have evolved over the millennia through intricate social interactions. Furthermore, one cannot by choice simply create another way of conceiving the social world because that world is constituted, is shaped already, by these inherited understandings. That is not to say that such under-standings do not evolve. Quite clearly they do – but it is an evolution rather than a deliberate recreation, albeit hastened by a critical tradition to which individuals contribute. Furthermore, that critical tradition will be fuelled by *discoveries within*, or new understandings of, that social reality which we have inherited. Thus, for example, a feminist perspective may argue, in the light of facts which are uncovered, that the family is (or is often) an oppressive social force. Recognition of this may lead to a reconceptualization of 'family'. But such a reconceptualization presupposes a social reality that exists independently of our choice or whim, even though that reality is constituted by social under-standings which could have been otherwise. To quote Bhaskar (1989, p. 4) in his interestingly named book *Reclaiming Reality*, 'Society then is the ensemble of positioned practices and networked interrelationships which individuals never create but in their practical activity always presuppose, and in so doing everywhere reproduce or transform.' Indeed, it is precisely this transforming nature of how people conceive social activities, sometimes deliberately pursued, which is so important in understanding what is happening in education and how one might conceptualize that which is to be researched into. There is a systematic attempt, as we saw in chapter 2, by those who manage the system to conceive education in managerial and business terms. And the resistance to this must be that the social practice of education – real and independent of the whims of the managerial class – cannot in justice be so described. If only the self-styled radicals of educational research, who subscribe to the equal validity of each person's socially constructed reality, would realize the justification they are providing to the Orwellian managers who seek to transform our understanding of education to their own image and likeness.

The realism, however, which I argue for, must not be confused with the 'naïve realism' which so many critics have in mind. 'Naïve realism' is the view that there is a one-to-one relation between our description of reality and reality itself – that our language, as it were, mirrors reality. It is as though we see reality as it is, unmediated by the language and concepts we have inherited. That is not my view. Rather must one recognize that, however culturally specific any one description of reality is, such a description has to come up against the hard facts of reality. Different cultures might mark out different ways of conceptualizing reality. But the viability of those distinctions depends upon features of the world which makes them possible. New Labour is a clear example of 'social construction' of reality, and many people are employed to construct that reality to suit the purposes of the politicians. 'Illness', 'waiting lists', 'investment in health service', 'expansion of provision' are constantly being 'reconstructed'. But every so often a hard-nosed realist asks 'where are the extra beds?' or points out that people have *really* died.

Realism in this sense provides the basis upon which one might distinguish between objective and subjective accounts. 'Objective' has a range of interconnected meanings. First, it signifies that what is said is in tune with the world as it really is; it is not the product of my (purely subjective) whim or wishes. Second, an enquiry is 'objective' in that it takes the necessary and appropriate steps to get at that objective state of affairs. That is, one sticks to the proper procedures, which are likely to arrive at the correct conclusions. Such objective approaches depend on the nature of the enquiry. But they include, for example, examination of the evidence, testing one's conclusions against experience, ensuring that the account is coherent and not self-contradictory, subjecting it to the critical scrutiny of others. To be objective is not the same as being correct. One could take all the steps which, in normal circumstances, would lead to the correct answer but still get it wrong. In the same way one might arrive at the right conclusions whilst being totally subjective. 'Objectivity' refers to the way one proceeds, given that it is possible to give an account of an objective state of affairs – that is, a state of affairs which *really* exists independently of my wishing it to be so.

Causal explanation
One purpose of research (but not necessarily the only one) is to explain what is the case or what has happened. A reason for seeking explanations might be to predict what will happen in the future or what would happen if there were to be certain interventions. For example, an explanation might be sought for the low standards of literacy so that one might know what interventions (for example, a 'literacy hour') would improve the

overall standards. The recently established international Campbell Centre for social and educational research, based on the lessons to be learnt from the Oxford-based Cochrane Centre for medical research, emphasizes the importance of large-scale tests in which comparisons are made between control and experimental groups where there are closely controlled interventions.

Therefore, one obvious way of explaining what happens is to give 'the cause' – the particular intervention, say, which makes the difference. And, indeed, causal explanation is associated with the first paradigm outlined in chapter 3. But it is not as easy as it seems to say what one means by a 'cause'. Let us consider the following example:

The cause of low achievement is basically economic – poverty. Therefore, if you want to raise achievement, you need to improve economic conditions.

This proposition makes a connection between two general states of affairs – poverty and low achievement – such that, given certain conditions (namely, those of poverty) then certain consequences will inevitably follow (namely, low achievement). There is a general law-like statement to the effect that, whenever conditions prevail of type C, then there will be events of type E. And this is similar to the kind of law-like statement which characterizes science. Take, for example, Boyle's Law, which says that the volume of a confined gas varies inversely with its pressure at a constant temperature. Thus, given standard conditions S (constant temperature), then whenever there is an instance of C (increased pressure of gas) there will be an instant of E (decreased volume of gas). Therefore, the one (the increase of pressure) might be said to cause the other (the decrease in volume).

There are, however, difficulties which need to be noted. Thus a distinction needs to be made between correlation and causal explanation. Indeed, it is often argued that all we can establish is a correlation and that no conclusions can be drawn about causality. However, a distinction can and must be made. Take for example the correlation between educational achievement and attending certain sorts of schools. It might be concluded that attendance at those schools was a causal factor in that achievement. However, there could be the counter argument that, with those pupils, there would have been high achievement even if they had not been to that sort of school. They had been selected, say, because of their parental support or their measured intelligence or their motivation. These were the significant factors in their achievement, which had nothing to do with the type of school, despite the strong correlation between achievement and type of school.

Therefore, we need to reformulate our expression of *causal* connection so that it is more than a statement of correlation. X can be said to be the cause of Y if, whenever an event of type X occurs and conditions of type C prevail, then an event of type Y occurs, together with the claims, first, that if X were not to occur then Y would not occur either, and, second, that if Y did not occur then X would not have occurred either. Thus, there is not only a strong correlation between events of a certain kind; there is also a relation of necessary and sufficient condition. Given condition C, then X is sufficient for Y to have occurred, and Y is necessary for saying that X occurred.

There are, however, still difficulties in this attempt to formulate a causal relationship. Let us consider this second example:

> The cause of John's success, despite family poverty which normally would explain low achievement, was sheer hard work. If he had not worked so hard, he would have failed like every one else on the estate.

Here we have an exception to the general law. And, critics would point out, there are so many such exceptions that it would be wrong to say that poverty causes failure. Indeed, so it is argued, it is the false belief in causality which has undermined the confidence of teachers and learners alike in what might be achieved. Pupils have been written off because of their economic and social background. The same 'determinism' that characterizes our understanding of the physical world has wrongly entered into educational practice.

The first point to be made is that there are many exceptions to the law-like statements of science. The generalities are maintained only in highly standardized conditions which do not prevail always in the real world. There are other interrelated events which complicate the conditions. Hence, scientists are constantly trying to understand the exceptions to the general laws without rejecting those laws themselves – although, if there are too many exceptions, the general explanatory laws might be superseded. Thus, in the case of John, it would be quite compatible to see an established connection between poverty and achievement whilst recognizing that in certain conditions that connection would not apply. Other law-like statements might be evoked to explain the exceptions – in this case concerning the impact of hard work in a well-motivated student. *In this respect* there seems to be no logical difference between general causal explanations in the sciences and general causal explanations in educational practice.

Furthermore, where a particular cause does not materialize, another might take its place. Hard work might be a causal factor in John's success. But had he not worked hard, another intervening factor might have replaced it and had the same effect – let us say, the particular attention of a brilliant teacher. Thus, we cannot get away from the idea of a causal factor rather than a mere correlation between two sorts of events. That is because the social world we are dealing with in educational practice has such a complicated set of interacting causal factors that we cannot isolate the events under consideration from this complex reality. There can never be the laboratory purity of the scientific world where standard and limited conditions can be assured.

Once one concedes there to be a social reality, not of our creation and not fully understood, there is no a priori reason why there should not be causal links between social facts and social structures, on the one hand, and how people behave or achieve or aspire, on the other. Such a causal link will of course, when expressed in general terms, be provisional and tentative because there are so many other factors which influence what happens. Hence, we want to cling on to the significance of such generalizations, whilst recognizing that they only apply in certain conditions – which conditions we might not fully understand. Connections can be made of a causal nature, even if such connections often fail because of other causes which get in the way. Such causal connections must not be so easily written off by politicians, who wish to put the blame for failure entirely in the hands of the teachers, or the 'social constructivists of multiple realities' – strange bedfellows, indeed.

However, there is a further argument, which complicates our understanding of causal explanation of social events. Thus, what I have explained above would support the view that, difficult though it is, one might specify the conditions wherein, more often than not, intervention X will cause event Y to occur. I say 'more often than not' because, as explained, other unpredictable causal events might occur and interfere. Thus, hard work and good teaching might generally lead to examination success, but unpredictably a bout of flu might intervene, accounting for poor results. None the less, despite such complications, such a causal account would seem to support the idea of a science of teaching. Once the government knows the right interventions to make (the right levers to pull or the right buttons to press) then it will be able to ensure higher performance against agreed standards (see Reynolds, 1998, for a confident appeal to such an idea).

However, it is argued that the complex world of social interactions makes such a science not just difficult but logically impossible. According to Luntley (2000, p. 17) in his criticism of performance-related pay, 'Classrooms (and other educational units) share a common structural feature with other social and natural systems – namely, non-linearity. Ignore this and you get a faulty logic of understanding for the system at issue.' With particular reference to economics (see Ormerod, 1998), Luntley argues that such are the interactions between elements in complex systems that it is impossible to predict what will happen. There is an ongoing 'dynamic effect' of each element on the other. 'Input X may on one occasion result in output Y, but that does not mean it will next time, for in the meantime responses from other elements in the environment may change the effect which X produces next' (Luntley, 2000, p. 18).

Hence, understanding complex systems (in this sense) is not the same as understanding the causal relations as I have explained them – even allowing for other intersecting causal influences. Because of the interactions between the different elements in the different causal chains, the overall set of interactions cannot produce a stable system which can be used by the gurus and bureaucrats of government to say with confidence what teachers must do to teach successfully.

However, there remains a further reason for doubting the application of the model of causal explanation, found in the sciences, to our understanding of individual or social action. It is not just a matter of the unpredictable nature of the interaction of the various elements in the causal systems. It is a matter of some of these elements being of a distinctive kind.

Explaining human behaviour

The question is whether there is something so distinctive about explaining human behaviour that the kinds of causal explanations which are applicable in science are inappropriate.

Quite influential educational research did assume that there was no reason why the science of physical phenomena should not be extended to an understanding of human behaviour. Skinner's theory of learning and its application to classrooms is an obvious example. His theory of operant conditioning, based on carefully controlled experiments with rats and pigeons, explains human behaviour in terms of reinforcement. Thus, behaviours, which initially might be random, eventually become strongly associated with specific 'rewards'. They no longer remain random. They are reinforced through constant association with certain conditions. A strong correlation is established between a particular kind of behaviour and a specific set of conditions, such that the latter might be seen to condition or to cause the former. Indeed, general law-like statements are established on the basis of many observed connections, and these can be verified by further observations. This kind of explanation requires the reduction of complex human activities to precise, observable and measurable units of behaviour.

The psychological explanation in terms of operant conditioning suggests ways of managing behaviour and classrooms. Thus, in order to ensure 'on-seat behaviour', such behaviour is associated with certain rewards. After a time, the temporarily modified behaviour becomes more permanent. There is a modification of behavioural habits. Indeed, there is now a 'science of behaviour modification'. Such a science assumes that human beings are simply what can be observed, that what they do can be spelt out in terms of observable behaviours, and that these behaviours can be adequately described and explained in terms of general law-like statements. No reference needs to be made to cognition, consciousness or intentions. These are part of the 'black box' which can be ignored as irrelevant in any attempts to understand and explain. Explanation lies in discovering the systematic connections between certain observable behaviours and certain conditions. On the basis of this knowledge, the teacher is able to intervene in order to ensure that behaviours are modified. (See Gurney, 1980, for a clear account of behaviour modification.)

There are, however, philosophical difficulties in this account of human behaviour. Imagine the sight of someone with the right arm uplifted. That might be fully described behaviourally – and agreement obtained from all onlookers. But it remains open to ask what is happening or what is that person doing. Various answers might be given. The person may be stretching because he is tired. He may be giving some pre-arranged signal to some friends. He may be seeking attention from passers by. He may be practising a special salute. The same *behaviour* might be any one of several possible actions – each one requiring a different sort of explanation. The point is that it is not possible to give an account of what people do without reference to the intentions which make that behaviour intelligible. This creates a sharp contrast between explanations of events in the physical world and explanations of human activities and behaviour. Physical objects do not interpret the world as a prelude to what happens to them. Human beings do and their behaviours can be understood only in terms of their intentions and thus their understanding of the physical and social worlds they inhabit.

Those intentions, as I said, require the agent to have an understanding of the world in which he is acting. The man signalling believes that there is at least one other who will interpret his behaviour in the way he wishes. There is an assumed social code wherein this behaviour takes on a particular significance. To practise a salute assumes a social practice in which saluting makes sense. Therefore, to explain human behaviour requires not only reference to the intentions of the person acting (as though these were within a purely private and subjective world), but also reference to the social rules and practices within which those intentional actions take place and make sense.

Let us take the example of the teacher who groups her students in a particular way. Those who want to make a science of teaching will look at how such observable behaviour does or does not, generally speaking, lead to certain outcomes. And, in the light of such a 'science of teaching', educational administrators may feel confident in prescribing how students should be grouped and how teachers should teach. But, of course, such 'observable behaviour' can be interpreted in many different ways, depending on the intentions of the teacher. What appear on the surface to be the same behaviours might well be quite different actions. The teacher's action might properly be described as 'organizing the class for reflective discussion' because that is the teacher's intention. But even that might not be enough. The mode of discussion, intended by the teacher, is part of a wider set of intentions in which controversial issues, say, become a central focus of the curriculum and in which discussion *of a certain sort* is thought to be essential. It is not possible to understand this teacher's behaviour without reference, not only to the immediate intention, but also to the wider understanding of this intentional action within a broader purposeful activity. To understand that activity one asks why the teacher is behaving in the way she is. The answer will not be in terms of causes in the scientific sense but in terms of how the teacher sees what she is doing in the light of a wider set of purposes. And indeed that will finally reveal her understanding of what she is doing as part of a social or educational practice. There would be some underlying view about the aims and values of education. These may not be shared by all teachers and hence they would need to be explained and justified to those who have a different 'philosophy' – a different conception of an 'educational practice'.

Moreover, for the teacher to succeed, the students will need to interpret her instructions and to understand the purposes which lie behind them. Indeed, an important element in teaching is to initiate the learners into a set of social practices, defined in terms of implicit rules of procedure and underlying aims and values. The students are entering into a social world shared with their teacher. To explain what is happening requires going beyond reference to immediate intentions. It requires also an account of that social world with its rules and values and its shared understandings.

We are seeing, therefore, that explaining human behaviour is not a simple matter. On the one hand, there are causal explanations which see that what people do or achieve is the product of social conditions. On the other hand, seemingly contradicting this, is explanation in terms of intentions and of the social rules and practices within which those intentions are intelligible and comprehensible to others. It is no good instructing the students to do something unless it is assumed that the students understand the nature and the purpose of the instructions. Explanation therefore incorporates both the intentions of the agent and the social rules and aims which make such intentions intelligible.

But reflection upon our common sense ways of explaining human behaviour reveals an even more complicated picture than what has been outlined so far. Thus it is perfectly sensible to explain how a person behaves in terms of their *motives* which are different from intentions. One might intend to punish a student from a sense of retribution or from anger or from spite. Furthermore, one might explain how a person behaves from their *dispositions to behave* in a certain way in particular circumstances. A kind person tends to act kindly; a brave person tends to act bravely when danger is lurking. And there might well be a causal explanation for the acquisition of particular dispositions.

Similarly a particular action might partly be explained in terms of the *capacities* of the agent. For example, he or she may have had diminished capacity for undertaking the activity or for under-standing the instructions. Causal explanations would here have a place. Capacities are affected by the ingredients of food, by exposure to polluted air, by the material quality of life.

How, then, might one summarize this rather complicated account of explanation? Is there a complete separation of the causal explanations, which one might give of the physical world, and the intentional explanations, which one gives of the personal and social world? Is it true that the mutually exclusive paradigms outlined in chapter 3 reflect the incompatibility between two radically different sorts of explanation?

First, it needs to be asserted that, even within the explanations which refer to the intentions of the agent, the picture is much more complicated than is often assumed. Explanations need to take into account the intentions of the agent, the wider understandings of the agent of both the physical and social world, the social practices in which those intentions are intelligible, the motives, capacities and the dispositions of the agent.

Second, however, those social practices, rather than being the creation of the agent, have a history, which needs to be understood and explained – the incorporation of a set of ideas which reflect deeper views of human nature. And, indeed, it is an important job of philosophy of education to make explicit the different traditions implicit within the different social practices in which education is to be understood. Take, for example, the social practice within schools of discussing controversial issues in the light of appropriate evidence (that is, the practice of discussing such issues through attending systematically to the arguments and evidence on both sides of the case). This social practice might be seen and understood within a broader but quite distinctive tradition of education. Such a tradition incorporates an understanding of how the teacher might proceed in exploring certain issues, or in conducting enquiries, whilst not claiming to be an authority on the correct resolution of those enquiries. The tradition behind the practice of such open-ended but systematic and evidence-based enquiry embodies a tentative attitude towards the teaching of values in a pluralist society. Such a tradition is argued for in the work of Stenhouse (see, in particular, his *Culture and Education*, 1967). Or one might think, too, of the practice in which the 'interests' of the learner play a determining role in the shaping of learning; such a practice has to be understood within a particular tradition of child-centred education (see Wilson, P., 1967).

Third, however, this essential reference to the intentions of the agent and the wider social practices which make those intentions intelligible, does not exclude the role of causal explanations in the more traditional sense of law-like statements which explain the particular in terms of the general and which facilitate predictions. Our understanding of others, however different they are in some respects and whatever cultural differences give rise to different social practices, presupposes some commonality. There is and must be some underlying view of human nature, which enables us to make assumptions about human dispositions and motivation (in terms of fear, ambition, self-preservation, etc.). There are connections, which we can identify, between social structures we have inherited and ways in which we have come to understand the world and our place within it. Our intentional behaviour does not occur within a cultural and social vacuum, and connections of a general kind can be made between the two, even if the agent, precisely through becoming conscious of those connections, is thus empowered to transcend or transform them. The background knowledge of social context or structure is a kind of causal factor as it enters into the determining intentions of the agent. But this will only explain what happens in a tentative and provisional way, since the growing consciousness of the learner enables him to overcome what otherwise would be determinants of his behaviour.

Truth

The mention of 'truth' or 'true' is often accompanied by the speaker indicating the use of quotation marks with their fingers in the air. It is as though it is a naughty word, which ought not to be used but which cannot be avoided. Hence, it is used on sufferance. This is reflected in the references I gave to Guba and Lincoln, who refer to a 'new construction' emerging through evaluation or research 'that is not better or truer'. And, indeed, the 'fourth generation of evaluation' finds any reference to 'truth' or 'true' exceedingly difficult to stomach. This reflects an anxiety which is widespread amongst educational researchers.

What then are the problems and the issues?

'True' is a predicate of a proposition or of several propositions, as in an argument. We say that it is *true* that the conditions in the school are not conducive to learning or that class size affects the quality of learning. By saying that these propositions are *true*, we indicate that, given the meanings of these words or symbols, then there is a state of affairs in the real world which they reflect accurately. There is some correspondence between the statements I utter and the world which exists independently of me. Traditionally this has been referred to as the 'correspondence theory of truth', and it is the nearest to what most people at the common sense level would accept. Language in some sense 'mirrors' reality. There is an isomorphic relation between the words we use and what those words signify. Take the example shown. There would

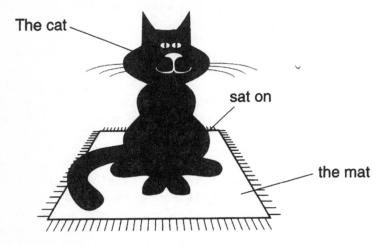

seem to be a one-to-one relationship between the word 'cat' and the actual cat, the word 'mat' and the actual mat, and the words 'sat on' and the actual relation between the cat and the mat. Furthermore, we can test or verify whether the proposition is an accurate reflection of reality by going out and having a look. If we were to observe a quite different relation of cat to mat (for example, if the cat were standing on the mat) then the proposition would be false.

There are some well-rehearsed objections to such a theory of truth. It rests on a theory of meaning, namely, that the meaning of a word is what it refers to. It is as though all nouns are really proper names. But that clearly is not the case. 'Cat' cannot *mean* this or that cat, because we come to refer to other creatures as cats not yet born. But, more importantly for educational research, how we in fact describe the world (for example, by using words like dogs and cats, puppies and kittens) could conceivably have been otherwise. There are many different ways in which we might have described or conceptualized what we see to be reality. This is why many want to say that such a description may be true for one person but not for another, or for one culture but not for another. Thus, it might be claimed by Mr Jones not to be true for him that class 5a is badly behaved; he would prefer to describe what class 5a do as 'lively' or 'high-spirited'.

There are other problems, too, with a correspondence theory of truth expressed in this way. How could you say that counterfactual conditional statements are true or false – that is, statements which say what would have happened if something had been the case (for example, 'if one had planned your lessons that way, then there would have been chaos')? What about mathematical statements, the truth or falsity of which depends on logical consistency rather than on correspondence with reality? Furthermore, what is the reality which would correspond to statements of value of the kind 'that was an elegantly delivered lesson' or 'it is wrong to beat children'? And yet we do argue about such statements; we do assume in everyday, common sense discourse that such statements might be untrue or need justification.

There are, therefore, difficulties in saying what one means when one says that a statement is true, and yet it seems impossible to get away from the notion – even if one carefully avoids using that word. Thus, when someone asserts something (such as 'there is no such thing as truth' or that 'what is true for you is not necessarily true for me'), it always makes sense to argue with the statement. It would make sense to deny what has been said. But to do this is to concede that what was said might be wrong and that its negation would be correct. Otherwise, what is the point of disagreeing or arguing? Or what is the point of asserting a point of view in the first place? In other words, one is back to the seemingly unavoidable position that statements are either true or false. To assert something, or to argue a point, is to assume that there are conditions ('truth conditions') which make that statement either true or false.

There might of course be very different kinds of truth conditions. They may be different for mathematical or purely logical statements than they are for statements about the physical world. They may be very different again for statements about morality or about religion or about persons. The point is that to enter into conversation is to assume that there are certain conditions which, if they prevail, make one's statements true – or make them false.

There are two common confusions, however, which need to be examined. The first is the confusion between verification and truth conditions. Thus, one may not be able to verify that a statement is true, but that does not prevent it from being true. By their very nature counterfactual conditionals cannot be verified. But, if certain conditions had prevailed, then it must be either true or false that certain consequences would have happened. Or one may not be able to verify the claim 'all children are inherently good', but, given agreement on what one means by these terms, then such a statement must be either true or false. Of course, disagreement may be so widespread about the meaning of these terms and about what would count as evidence for or against, that one would want to say that the words 'all children are inherently good' are simply meaningless. It is a set of words with all the grammatical properties of a meaningful proposition, but, since no one knows what on earth follows from its being uttered, it makes no sense at all.

The second confusion mixes disagreement over appropriate description of reality with a rejection of the claim that statements are either true or false. The same situation can be described differently according to the purpose of the description. Thus, a particular incident in the class might equally validly be described as an intelligent or a rude response to the teacher. Indeed, both may be correct descriptions – one can be intelligently rude. On the other hand, one way of describing the incident, given what is generally meant by 'rude', may be quite inappropriate. Following further investigation into the motives of the student, etc., then one has to withdraw the claim that he was rude. Of course, describing social reality is much more complicated than that. But disagreement is not simply about whether a given claim is true or false, but also about whether a particular way of describing reality is an appropriate one or not. And, indeed, that is the very stuff of educational argument, as one person or group tries to persuade others of a different way of seeing things in the light of further evidence. One might resist, for example, the description of people as intelligent or not in the light of the many ways in which people deal intelligently with different situations and problems.

Therefore, in rejecting a 'picture theory of meaning', in which a statement is true or false depending on whether it 'mirrors' accurately the real world, one still cannot get rid of the central element of the correspondence theory of truth. That central element is that the truth or falsity of what is said has something to do with a reality which is independent of the statements made about it. Such reality firmly resists certain descriptions of it. We might legitimately for different purposes describe the world in many different ways. But, for those descriptions and distinctions to stick, there must be features of that world which enable them to be made. One cannot get away from reality – and thus from the truth or falsity of statements which give an account of it.

Bridges (1999) gives an excellent taxonomy of the different

theories of truth which have an impact upon the conduct of educational research. He distinguishes between correspondence, coherence, pragmatic, consensus and warranted belief theories of truth. But in setting out the various pros and cons of each, he fails to recognize the inevitable correspondence between what is said and what *is*, even if that correspondence is not of the simplistic kind outlined in 'picture theory of meaning'. Realism and accounts of reality and truth are inseparable, and failure to recognize that leads to strange and indefensible consequences in the theory and practice of research.

Facts

Perhaps another way of thinking about 'truth' is to think about what are 'facts', though this concept seems to be as elusive as 'truth'. And yet, certainly at the common sense level, we talk quite happily about facts. When there has been a disturbance, the head teacher quite properly asks for the facts (as opposed to the fictitious accounts which some may be giving). General claims about school performance, say, need to be checked against the facts.

The difficulty lies in associating 'facts' with discrete events, which correspond to the discrete statements supposedly mirroring or picturing them. Thus, a full description of Budleigh Salterton beach in Britain would, on this view, pick out all the facts – statements about the millions of multi-coloured pebbles which constitute that beach. But that cannot be acceptable. There are many different ways in which that beach could be described – each of which could be factually correct. Just as language about reality cannot be broken down into a finite set of basic statements, so reality is not made up of a large but finite set of facts to which these basic statements correspond. But that, as I have explained, does not entail that there are not features of that reality which enable us correctly to say certain sorts of things. 'Facts' refer to those features of reality, described in one way rather than another, which enable us truthfully to make certain statements.

Facts, therefore, are not the sorts of things which one observes independently of a particular way of describing the world. A different way of describing the world would appeal to different facts. But facts they remain, reflecting features of a real world which limit what could be an appropriate description.

There seems, therefore, no reason why one should not talk of *social* facts, that is, those features of the social world which make statements about that world either true or false. Thus, as I explained above, there are aspects of the personal and social worlds which are not of my personal creation, even though they are the result of social interactions and even though they might be transformed through further personal and social deliberations. I inherit a social world through which relationships are established and recognized. I, along with others, make discoveries within that social world. And, having discovered them, I can change that world – alter the facts, if you like.

Facts, therefore, do not stare you in the face, impressing themselves upon you. They are not the sort of *thing* which can be collected and added up. Rather are they identified within a particular way of describing the physical and social worlds. The head teacher, ascertaining the cause of the trouble, has already delineated what are to count as facts, namely, those events (those aspects of the real world, including social relationships) which help explain a particular sort of event. If you like, what constitutes 'the facts' is already 'theory laden'. 'Facts', theory and descriptions of reality are interconnected concepts.

Partly because this has not been recognized, and thus partly because the facts are seen to be discrete and observable events or things in the real world, a clear distinction is made between fact and value. It is claimed that no amount of facts about the real world entails how one ought to act within it. The radical distinction between fact and value receives its most forceful and famous expression in Hume's *Treatise of Human Nature*, where he argues that you cannot derive an 'ought' from an 'is'. No amount of factual statements entails what one ought to do. Statements of duty or right or goodness or value are quite separate from statements of what is the case. And for many philosophers, this separation of fact from value led to pure subjectivism as far as any evaluation was concerned or, indeed, to the reduction of evaluations (aesthetic, moral, political, etc.) to mere expressions of emotion (Ayer, 1946, chapter 6). Realism, certainly, but only in matters which can be empirically investigated, not in matters of value.

The radical separation of fact from value is difficult to maintain, especially since facts relate to the descriptions we give of the world and those descriptions incorporate evaluations. Take, for example, research into health. What constitutes a healthy person is not a straightforward empirical matter. It depends on the values one has. People will disagree over levels of fitness which constitutes a healthy person, and those differences will relate to more general beliefs about quality of life. This is clear where one has in mind mental health. But it applies, too, to physical health. And so systematic reviews of educational research into such matters as bullying would need to bear in mind that different researchers will start from different definitions of 'bullying' as they evaluate differently various incidents. Values permeate our descriptions of reality.

Theory

Secretaries of State, politicians and the various lobby groups which advise them are against theory. The Secretary of State for Education in Britain, in response to the research of Farrow, Tymms and Henderson (1999), which demonstrated that assumptions about the value of homework should not automatically be grafted on to primary practice, said 'Some researchers are so obsessed with "critique", so out of touch with reality that they churn out findings which no one with the slightest common sense could take seriously' (Blunkett, 1999). And so theoretical work is called to account before the court of common sense. So too with the preparation of teachers. Theory is seen as a disease, which has to be eradicated and replaced by professional judgement. This is gained from practical experience.

But it is rarely clear what people are against when they dismiss theory. It is important to distinguish between theory, in the sense of the assumptions which lie behind practice but which often go unacknowledged, and theory, in the sense of tightly organized systems of explanation which are contrasted with the common sense referred to by the Secretary of State.

It is common now to say that all observations are theory laden. By that is meant that what we observe depends upon the concepts and beliefs which we bring to those observations. Those concepts and those beliefs, in the common sense world Mr Blunkett refers to, are rarely made explicit. But they are there none the less – beliefs about children's motivation, about the righteousness and effectiveness of punishment, about the value of learning this rather than that, even about the nature and quality of educational research. Such a framework of ideas and beliefs is not, as it were, in the world waiting to be absorbed. It is what we bring to our observations of that world. It shapes the observations we make. To make these underlying assumptions explicit is to reveal a framework of beliefs and ideas which might or might not be called theory, depending upon its level of reflection and articulation. Furthermore, once articulated and subject to criticism, one's common sense views may seem not to be common sense after all.

Therefore, to think of practice apart from theory (of some sort) is to create another false dualism. The dualism is created by the examination of theory as such and by asking how this or that theory relates to practice, as though practice were standing outside a theoretical framework. On the contrary, to look at practice, to see how it is always open to a further account of what is being practised and thus to the possibility of questions being raised which can be treated more theoretically, implies the logical inseparability of theory from practice.

Theory here, then, refers to the articulation of the framework of beliefs and understandings which are embedded in the practice we engage in. Such a theoretical position may be expressed in everyday, non-theoretical language. But, none the less, it is what we bring to our observation of the world and to the interpretation of those observations. It involves a more or less coherent account of the values and motivations, of human capacities and aspirations. And such an account, when articulated, is open to critical scrutiny.

In certain areas of observation, however, that framework of ideas and that critical scrutiny of received assumptions have taken flight from common sense. The well-established belief that the earth goes round the sun, not vice versa, went against common sense beliefs. The theoretical language of science is not that of everyday discourse. It has to be learnt as a new language.

This connection between theory and common sense I shall examine in greater detail in the section below (see Common Sense Explanations). It is important to get it right. We need to ask how far research should employ the more theoretical language of specialist disciplines, thereby distancing itself from the everyday discourse of the teacher, and how far it might remain within that discourse with all its imprecision and ambiguities. But the important thing to remember at this stage of the argument is that the much despised theory, in the sense of a framework of concepts and beliefs, far from being quite separate from practice, is the articulation of what is implicit in practice. Those who want researchers to cut the theory and simply to say 'what works', forget that what counts as 'working' makes many unquestioned assumptions that need to be examined.

Knowledge

A criticism of educational research is that it does not create a body of knowledge upon which policy-makers and professionals can rely. First, a lot of the research is small scale and fragmented and there is no cumulative growth of such knowledge. Second, educational discourse seems to be full of people criticizing others' research such that there is nothing conclusively verified – no *knowledge*. Research conclusions seem more like transient beliefs than well-established knowledge.

One philosophical analysis of knowing that something is the case goes like this. 'X knows that P' (where P stands for any statement) if, and only if, (i) X believes that P, (ii) X is justified in believing that P, and (iii) P is true. (See for variations of this analysis Ayer, 1956; Scheffler, 1965; Woozley, 1949.) For example, a teacher's claim to know that a pupil would do well in examinations is refuted if (i) the teacher demonstrates lack of belief by giving basic remedial lessons, or (ii) the grounds for believing it were mistaken – he was confusing the student's work with someone else's, or (iii) the student eventually failed the examinations. The teacher had a tentative but mistaken belief; but he lacked knowledge.

To claim that I know something to be the case does imply that I could have been wrong but that, in the light of relevant evidence or argument, I have good reason for so believing. Furthermore, it turns out that I was not wrong. The proposition 'P' was true. Thus, 'knowledge' would, on this analysis, be logically related to 'truth' and, indeed, to a 'reality' which makes my claim a true one and to a mode of enquiry and verification which constitutes, objectively speaking, a justification for that belief. Knowledge is not a description of a psychological state of mind – a strong belief. It depends on a publicly agreed framework of justification, refutation and verification.

Therefore, there is a slightly different, though obviously related, sense of knowledge. We talk of 'bodies of knowledge'. This takes the emphasis away from this or that person's state of mind. Indeed, one might refer to the accumulation of such knowledge in libraries or data bases even though no one person is in possession of it. Knowledge without a knower. One could imagine the almost total obliteration of the human race but not the knowledge which is stored away in filing cabinets and books, awaiting rediscovery by the few survivors. Popper (1972) refers to this as the 'third world' – the first being my mental state and beliefs and the second being the reality which exists independently of those mental states. The problems in failing to recognize this 'third world' are that, first, 'knowledge' comes to be associated with the private beliefs of each individual and, second, the justification of a knowledge claim would lie in linking these subjective states of mind to the objective reality. And that problem is reflected in Descartes' search for the indisputable proposition through the process of methodological doubt to what simply cannot be doubted.

These 'bodies of knowledge' are the theories, propositions and explanations which have accumulated through enquiry, criticism, argument and counter argument. They are what have survived testing and criticism. They are, as it were, public property. And indeed their credentials depend upon their being open to public challenge and refutation. Hence, any 'body of knowledge', though well corroborated, can only be provisional; it is open to further change through criticism. The link between 'knowledge' and 'certainty' is broken. The strength of one's belief and the sense of certainty are no guarantee of knowledge. Indeed, there can be no basis for certainty; it is always conceivable that what one believes might turn out to be wrong in the light of further experience and criticism.

It is the job of the teacher to enable the young learner to get a grasp of these publicly developed bodies of knowledge, thereby transforming their subjective representations of the world. By 'getting a grasp' of a form or body of knowledge I mean coming to understand the key ideas or concepts which are embodied within it, the modes of enquiry through which they are developed, the tests for truth and validity. And this, as Bruner (1960) so well argued, can begin in an intellectually respectable way at any age.

In failing to recognize this, one is in danger of undermining the authority and professional role of the teacher. The teacher is not paid to transmit his or her personal views and certainties. The teacher's authority lies in his or her mastery or grasp of the form or body of knowledge which he or she draws upon to enhance and form the judgement of the learner. The mathematician feels confident in her teaching because there is public testament to the fact that she has grasped the key elements in a distinctive body of knowledge. This is not a private game that she is playing. That is why the teaching of personal and social development is so difficult and unpopular. Where is the publicly agreed body of knowledge upon which the teacher can draw to inform the deliberations of the young learner? (It was for this reason that Stenhouse, in developing the Humanities Curriculum Project, insisted upon certain teaching strategies for the teaching of controversial issues of practical living (see Stenhouse, 1975).)

The question for educational research, therefore, is whether there is or could be a body of knowledge with its distinctive ideas and concepts, its general principles and theories, its peculiar modes of enquiry, its agreed tests of truth, which has accumulated and grown through criticism, experiment, testing, reflection and so on and which one might draw upon with confidence as policy-maker or professional in making decisions about what one ought to do. Such bodies of knowledge could be fairly low level and not very theoretical. They could contain generalizations on such matters as school effectiveness. They could, in borrowing from the social sciences, be theoretical in language and explanation.

But one criticism of educational research is that there do not seem to be such bodies of knowledge. There does not seem to be the long-term research programme in which new researchers build on the discoveries of the old. Who now reads Bruner or Peel? How far does present know-how build on the research of Piaget and Kohlberg? Have not the well-researched achievements of Stenhouse disappeared with his premature death – or will do with the death of his disciples? There is therefore an important question to be asked about the nature of professional judgment and the relation of that to the growth of knowledge through research.

* * *

I have articulated certain key and indispensable concepts in any understanding of research. The particular spin one gives these concepts affects profoundly the practice of research and the credence one gives its conclusions.

On the one hand, one can talk of the 'real world' to be researched into, existing independently of the researcher who will, following proper (objective) procedures, make statements which can be verified and thus shown to be true. Such truth depends on the facts which rather awkwardly determine what can be truthfully said. Furthermore, the accumulation of such true statements might lead to a coherent and explanatory system (a body of knowledge) which, in the light of further criticism and evidence, will constantly change. But that change will be a kind of growth, each succeeding stage incorporating but improving upon the previous one.

On the other hand, one cannot talk of reality independent of the researcher. 'Reality' is a social construction, and the boundaries between the objective and the subjective become blurred. There are as many realities as there are social constructions, which is a large number, indeed. The researcher becomes part of the world to be researched, and the truth is no longer a relation between statements and the facts which the statements are about, but rather a negotiated and agreed account of what should be regarded as real.

I, of course, wish to argue that it is more complicated than that. That is reflected in my analysis of these different concepts. I shall return to these constantly in the following chapters. But there is one matter which has cropped up constantly, namely, the place of common sense in the evaluation of what research says. For Mr Blunkett, research which did not measure up to common sense was surely to be rejected. But whose common sense did he have in mind? A consideration of this will help us to get closer to the nature of educational research – namely, the research which makes sense of educational practice.

COMMON SENSE EXPLANATIONS

Common sense beliefs are to be contrasted, on the one hand, with those which are theoretical and, on the other, with those which are self-evidently false. Common sense language is contrasted with the technical language through which experience is redescribed in a more precise and scientific manner. Philosophers were once fond of contrasting 'the world of science' with 'the everyday world' or 'technical' with 'untechnical' concepts (see Ryle, 1954). And so the contrast continues, and it is often the aim of educational researchers to inject into everyday discourse the more technical language of the social sciences. How else might one develop a science of teaching or of the effective school? And politicians and bureaucrats prefer that because such a language enables more exact accountability.

An example of this attempt to shift from the inadequacies of common sense to more scientific explanations, which, if true, should inform teaching, is that of Atkinson (1964). He argued that psychology (especially in its understanding of motivation) has, as an experimental science of behaviour, moved from the 'fund of pre-scientific, intuitive wisdom we call common sense through several stages of increased sophistication in methods of study'. Part of that increased sophistication is a more suitable conceptual scheme. Psychology aims to develop a conceptual or theoretical scheme, which explains more adequately than conventional wisdom 'the direction, vigour and persistence of an individual's action'. In pursuing this task, Atkinson finds such concepts as 'wants', 'wishes', 'desires', 'intentions' and 'purposes' unhelpful. They are imprecise and ultimately circular in definition. The development of psychology lies in a more tightly defined theoretical language such as that of psychoanalysis, neuro-physiology or behaviourism. These then become a substitute for how we ordinarily explain why people act as they do.

Atkinson is saying that how we ordinarily account for motivation is inadequate. Such accounts need to be superseded by a new language which draws the conceptual boundaries differently and makes different assumptions. But, in attempting to do this, Atkinson runs into difficulties, and an examination of these is revealing. The new, recommended language has to apply to something, and that something is the individual or group of individuals picked out within our ordinary or common sense discourse. The point of developing theories of motivation is to assist us in pursuing practical tasks such as teaching or solving practical problems such as classroom management that have been identified in the non-theoretical language of everyday living. The *solutions* posed in the language of behaviourism have to be connected with the *problems* posed in the language of 'wishes', 'wants', 'desires' and 'intentions'. To do this is to face the logical problem of relating a limited and technical universe of discourse to that which ordinary language users are familiar with. Perhaps that is why teachers find the 'thinking in business terms', with its definition of what they are doing in terms of targets, inputs, audits and performance indicators, so difficult to accept.

The problem, however, is not simply one of keeping in view the non-theoretical objects or events identified in common sense to which the theory must relate. The common sense account of things determines what sort of explanation is relevant. To identify a behaviour as someone's action (as opposed to a reflex or an involuntary act) is, as I explained in chapter 3, to see it within a framework of intentions, and of social rules that make those intentions intelligible. No adequate theoretical account can ignore this intentional and social dimension. If it did, what would it be explaining? We are committed to a certain kind of explanation, and that kind of explanation would exclude others (e.g. behavioural) if these were put forward as *complete* accounts of why people act as they do.

None the less, to talk of common understandings, common sense beliefs and the ordinary language of the ordinary person, or to talk of practical common sense, has its problems. It is not clear what is this 'common sense', or how it might relate to the non-common sense knowledge of theorists and researchers. Can we identify a sufficiently distinctive area of thought that might roughly be called common sense thinking? If so, what philosophical attitude should we adopt towards it – regarding it, on the one hand, as provisional and inadequate, or, on the other, as indispensable and as the touchstone of what is real and true? Certainly, it may constantly need to be refined, but not to be disposed of. What is the relation of such common sense thinking to the more disciplined thinking characteristic of a certain kind of research?

Common sense might be precisely what researchers want to challenge. It often refers to statements and explanations which are seen to be obviously true. Common sense is the range of unquestioned beliefs which groups of people share and which provide a basic view of the world – what Atkinson referred to as the 'fund of pre-scientific, intuitive wisdom'. It provides the rules of thumb whereby each person is able to live and make decisions. And probably it works well when the physical and social environments are sufficiently stable for the continued success of unquestioned assumption.

However, a feature of such common sense is its changing content. What is common sense at one time may no longer be so at another; what is not known at one time might become part of the unquestioned folklore later. Relating home environment to school performance is now part of teachers' common sense, although once this connection would not have seemed obvious. Research percolates down to the unquestioned assumptions of everyday life, thereby extending or changing common sense. Furthermore, one person's common sense may not be another's. The common sense beliefs of the teacher may not be obvious to the parent, so that the unquestioned assumptions of the one may be either incomprehensible or questionable to the other.

What picks out such beliefs as common sense is the *manner* in which they are held – unquestioningly, commonly held to be obvious. In this sense, research is at odds with common sense, not necessarily with its content (which may be true and significant) but with the unquestioning manner in which the beliefs are held. In developing a non-common sense attitude towards one's beliefs one is at the beginning of the disciplined, critical and reflective thinking that is the mark of educational research. The 'education of common sense' lies in the acquisition of mental habits and qualities – a questioning and critical approach to what was accepted uncritically, a refusal to accept as self-evident what is generally believed to be true, a reflective and analytic attitude towards the fund of inherited wisdom.

On the other hand, such common sense includes certain beliefs which seem undeniable – that there is an external world within which physical objects interact causally with one another and that there are persons who, with intentions and motives, are not reducible to physical objects. The feature of these more central common sense beliefs is not the *manner* in which they are held but their peculiar status. They are in one sense unquestionable for they contain presuppositions which are basic to all our thought. They provide a skeletal framework of beliefs which cannot be superseded by theoretical thinking. Indeed, it was with the development of such presuppositions that Piaget was concerned – the categorical framework that both precedes and enters into the more reflective states of theoretical thinking. Theoretical and more disciplined thinking of research could not contradict this 'common sense framework' of experience. Rather would it incorporate the common sense reference to objects and their qualities, and to persons and their motives, or (in the more formalized disciplines) construct for particular purposes new objects of references which none the less must be related back to the framework of common sense.

To summarize, common sense refers to several things. First, it refers to those beliefs which are held in an unquestioned way; such beliefs changing from group to group and from age to age. Second, it refers to the indispensable framework within which we identify and think about the physical world in time and space, cause and effect, and persons. Third, it refers to the shared discourse (which may be more or less sophisticated) which is to be contrasted with the more technical and limited forms of discourse of the physical and the social sciences.

Research is often a challenge to common sense in the first meaning. It questions what previously went unquestioned, and it might do so in the light of contrary evidence or of comparisons with what is believed elsewhere. Research is often, also, a challenge to common sense in the third meaning, in wanting to bring a more theoretical perspective from the social sciences to what previously had been understood in the looser, albeit more subtle, language of ordinary discourse. But these theoretical accounts cannot run too far away from the second meaning of common sense – namely, the necessary and basic framework of ideas about the physical, personal and social worlds in which we live.

It is necessary to say a little more about this contrast between a theoretical perspective, through which people claim to have understood the social world, and the everyday discourse through which we normally talk about it. One reason is that unless there can be a bridge between the common sense discourse and the more technical discourse, then theory-based research will have little or no impact upon policy or practice.

Let us take various examples of theory. At one extreme, theory is created and developed by dissenting from the postulates of everyday discourse. The physicist creates a different universe of discourse from that of visible, tangible objects, as it postulates instead non-sensible 'objects' like particles. Psychologists, like Skinner and Atkinson, postulate, contrary to common sense beliefs, that man is not to be understood as an intentional agent with wishes and wants. The world of economics is not fundamentally different from that of common sense – it assumes a world of persons with wants, wishes and intentions and makes certain assumptions (about the movement of prices, say) which the non-economist would recognize from everyday experience. But what is not common sense is the tidying up of these beliefs in the postulation, contrary to daily experiences, of the 'rational man', in the stipulation of greater conceptual precision, and in the quantification of relationships between different factors (as, for example, in showing by graphs the elasticity of supply and demand). To postulate such individuals as the 'rational man', to stipulate precise definitions of key terms, and to quantify relations between them depends on the acceptance of conventions which hang together as a system, certainly, but which are not part of common sense. 'Homo economicus', like 'homo Skinnerius', is an abstraction from the rather complex being we meet on the street or in literature.

Frequently connected with this limitation of the field of discourse is, as I have pointed out, a technical precision injected into the use of terms – as, for example, in reducing intentional actions to measurable behaviours. An ideal of the natural sciences would be the replacement of qualitative by quantitative descriptions wherever possible, as for instance in substituting precise standards of measurement for 'everyday judgements' of temperature. Such precision is demanded, too, in the social sciences, as when, for example, in psychology attitude tests are given, or deviations from the norm statistically expressed. Even where, as in non-scientific disciplines, quantification is clearly impossible, crucial terms are by definition rendered sufficiently precise that even these are marked off from their use (if they had one) in ordinary discourse.

Where common sense, therefore, refers to the uncritical *manner* in which beliefs are held, it needs to be superseded. But, in so far as such critical enquiry develops more theoretical precision, there arise logical differences between the *discourse* of common sense and that of theory. Common sense no longer refers simply to the uncritical manner in which beliefs are held. It refers to a structure of beliefs which, though they are to be contrasted with theory, seem to be more basic and for many purposes quite adequate. Such common sense needs to be rejected by researchers with caution. Without this link to such common sense, specialized thinking, with its technically defined terms and its restricted subject matter, would have no 'purchase' upon the questions we ordinarily ask. The teacher, caught in the complex practical world of the classroom, needs to see where the theoretical account latches on to his or her quite different universe of discourse. The theorist needs to show where theory corrects or improves the common sense beliefs that inform a teacher's practice.

The force of my argument has lain not simply on the contrast between common sense and the more disciplined and theoretical modes of thinking but also upon their interconnection. The language of everyday usage employs a range of concepts, principles, rules of inference for a multitude of overlapping purposes – a complex picture of the world within a framework of material objects and purposive, rule-following persons, of duties and rights and social interactions. And it is in this complex picture of the world that problems are first identified for research and theoretical treatment and that theory (often by concentration upon the quantifiable aspects of experience) injects some precision, whilst at the same time being placed in perspective. The framework of ordinary language, together with the accompanying beliefs about the external world, other minds, etc., provides both the starting point and the point of application of theory, the bridge between different disciplines, the common ground of intelligibility that enables communication between different theoretical accounts. Some logical priority must therefore be given to what Ryle calls 'the everyday world' and 'the concepts of everyday discourse'. It is important to bear in mind how psychological explanations of behaviour are connected with the language in which we ascribe motives and intentions, or how the formal and informal teaching styles of Bennett (1975) relate to the distinctions teachers make in describing their classrooms. Theory runs parallel with ordinary language (and is therefore a substitute for it) only for particular purposes. The language of atoms and particles needs to be related to the language of tables and chairs. The language of behaviour modification needs to be related to the language of intentions and motives. The language of school effectiveness needs to be related to the language of relationships and moral purposes. The language of attainment and competencies needs to be related to the language of understanding and knowledge, with all the complexity of which philosophers have reminded us from Plato onwards.

CONCLUSION

There are deep divisions between educational researchers based upon philosophical positions, which are rarely made explicit. Such differences, however, have a profound impact upon the conduct of research. I have tried to show how these philosophical differences refer to the interrelated concepts concerned with reality and objectivity, with truth, facts and verification, with theory and knowledge. These concepts, which seem indispensable in the discourse of research, are however applied with sufficient variation as to create very different ideas about the nature and the conduct of research. I have tried to show that in some cases the underlying philosophical positions are simply mistaken. Indeed, I have indicated that, in failing to do a proper philosophical job, educational researchers have drawn too sharp a contrast between quantitative and qualitative traditions. The way in which we understand and explain the social world, and thus educational practice, is more complex and subtle than that. That would be apparent if only educational researchers would attend more closely to how we do explain persons and social practice.

Part of the problem is a failure to attend to the rich and subtle ways in which we have come to describe social practice, embedded in the language of ordinary usage. Common sense beliefs need to be questioned, but the language of common sense embodies a complex way of understanding the world, which at one level is not to be dispensed with and at another level is the best that we have. Research has to relate back to it, and the philosophical under-pinnings of that research cannot ignore what common sense has to say about the reality to be researched into.

The position espoused here might be roughly described as one of robust realism, firmly rooted in the common sense language through which we have come to describe the natural and the social worlds we inhabit, and respecting therefore the logically different kinds of explanation which are embedded in that language. Beware of 'isms' – and of the distinctions which arise from their rigid application. Perhaps another way of looking at this is to examine some of these 'isms'. That I shall do in the next chapter.

Competing philosophical positions

The issues we have been dealing with – quantitative versus qualitative research, the nature of truth and its verification, what counts as reality, objectivity and subjectivity, knowledge and its growth, and so on – might fruitfully be approached from a different angle. Dominant ways of thinking about social phenomena have been defined through distinct theoretical positions. These positions are, as it were, the cultural and philosophical background against which research is conducted. Without the explicit formulation of the philosophical background – with implications for verification, explanation, knowledge of reality – researchers may remain innocently unaware of the deeper meaning and commitments of what they say or of how they conduct their research. (See, for example, Atkinson *et al.*, 1993.)

These philosophical positions are known by a range of bewildering titles. We hear of 'positivism' (which represents a philosophical tradition held in much contempt by many researchers), functionalism, interpretative theory, phenomenology, ethnomethodology, ethnography, constructivism, postmodernism, and so on. In the following sections, I attempt to provide a brief philosophical map of the dominant positions. But, of course, any map could have been drawn differently, making further distinctions and blurring others.

POSITIVISM

I start with 'positivism', not because chronologically it is prior. Philosophers from the presocratics onwards have provided nonpositivist explanations of how and why human beings behave in the way that they do. But, in the more recent and more self-conscious attempts to research personal and social behaviour, the positivist spirit has seemed to offer greater chance of progress. Indeed, criticism of educational research by those who want clear results on which they might base policy or practice would seem to share in this positivist spirit. And philosophically the recent history of educational research has been dominated by the apparent conflict between the positivist and interpretivist traditions.

The name which historically is most closely associated with positivism is Auguste Comte, a nineteenth-century French philosopher. But he himself was working within a tradition of empiricism, which would count amongst its adherents such British philosophers as Locke, Hume and Bacon. That tradition distrusted knowledge-claims which went beyond what was accessible to observation. It distrusted and rejected, therefore, philosophical and religious beliefs which gave a non-empirical account of the world. The word 'positivist' seems to refer to those accounts, which study systematically what is clear, factual and open to observation.

As we have seen, what count as facts, or what are basic objects of observation, are by no means unambiguous. Are they things like churches and schools? Or are they the bricks and mortar, which, put together, we (but possibly not others from a very different culture) call churches and schools? Or are they the uninterpreted experience of colours, shapes, sounds – the phenomena of direct experience? (See Ayer, 1963, for a thoroughgoing account of 'phenomenalism', according to which physical objects are constructions out of sense-data.) None the less, here was a *positive* account of that which needed to be understood. And the way of understanding was clearly that of the sciences, which had proved to be so productive in explaining phenomena and in predicting what is likely to happen in the future. A major contribution of Comte was the extension of this positivist agenda to the study and explanation of society, social structures and human affairs. A positivist account must embrace not only the phenomena of the physical world but also those of the social world in what was to be, in Carnap's words, a unity of the sciences. There was to be a science of society.

Those who now decry the positivist agenda need to remember the spirit and motives which drove it. There was a deep suspicion of those explanations, without evidence to support them and not open therefore to counter argument, which sustained the social order as it was, despite the obvious injustices and evils. Indeed, positivism took on the role of a religion. There were even temples to positivism; the London Positivist Society, founded in 1867, opened a positivist temple in Chapel Street in the east end of London. There was an almost religious fervour about the benefits which the proper study of society could bring to the improvement of society. Effective action required knowledge. And an important tradition of social research stemmed from those beliefs.

In more recent times, that positivist spirit and agenda were reflected in the pre-war work of the Vienna Circle, a group of philosophers united in what they believed to be meaningful beliefs about the world – what could count as intelligible knowledge of that world. It was best reflected in the work of one of its members, Rudolf Carnap. The foundation of all knowledge must be the immediate experiences that we have. Therefore, the theories and bodies of knowledge – which we develop – must ultimately be logically reducible to 'basic statements' about those experiences, even if, at first acquaintance, they do not *appear* to be about such experiences. How might one get out of this problem? The agenda set by the Circle was one of showing how all meaningful statements (in the sciences, say, or in the social studies) can be logically reduced to statements about immediate experiences. If they cannot be so reduced then they are pseudo-statements; we can forget about them. We have been deceived by the grammar of such statements as 'God is omnipotent' or 'We ought to pursue the general good of society' into believing that something meaningful has been said. However, since such statements cannot logically be reduced to statements about experience, they are not genuine statements at all.

Possibly the most influential exponent of this position in Britain was A. J. Ayer, who had briefly been a member of the Vienna Circle and who later became Professor of Philosophy at University College London and Wykeham Professor of Logic at the University of Oxford. In his book *Language, Truth and Logic*, first published in 1936, Ayer set out the logical principles of positivism – hence, the name 'logical positivism'. The central principle was that the meaning of a proposition lies in its mode of verification. Thus:

> We say that a sentence is factually significant to any given person, if, and only if, he knows how to verify the proposition which it purports to express – that is, if he knows what observations would lead him, under certain conditions, to accept the proposition as being true, or reject it as being false. (Ayer, 1946, p. 16)

It is important to attend carefully to this formulation and to understand the consequences. Let us forget for the moment exclamations of emotion, utterances of disgust, commands and orders, or requests of various kinds. Ayer argues that, in making a *statement*, one is claiming that something is the case. One is saying that the world, or whatever, has certain properties or features. For example, either it is or it is not raining; either I have or I do not have a broken leg; either the class is or it is not misbehaving. Of course, these concepts are blurred at the edges and there may be disagreement in definition. But such disagreement can be cleared up. And, once we are clear about the meaning of these terms, we know what sort of evidence would justify their application to experience. If there is simply no such evidence, no way of verifying the statement, then they are not genuine statements, whatever their grammatical form.

The consequences of this position are pretty drastic. According to Ayer, there are only two kinds of proposition which can be verified – and thus only two kinds of proposition which can be said to be meaningful. Those are empirical statements of the kind that science is built upon, and logical/mathematical statements which are true tautologically. If you want to know the truth of the statement ' it is raining', you go out and have a look or feel. If you want to know the truth of the mathematical statement '2 + 2 = 4' you refer to the meaning of the terms and the principle of contradiction. Ultimately all meaningful statements can be translated out into statements reporting experience or into statements which are *logically* correct. By this token, statements about what is right and good and beautiful, or about what one ought to do, have no meaning. There are no ways even in principle of verifying them. They are mere expressions of emotion. The statement 'you were wrong in punishing that child' is really a combination of the factual claim 'you punished that child' and an expression of emotion. (This has been called the 'boo-hurrah' theory of ethics.)

Science, therefore, shows the way for the development of knowledge. Its statements are verifiable. In making any claim, one knows what kind of evidence would verify or falsify what is said. The meaning of what is said is indeed the mode of verification. Scientific statements are verified differently from mathematical or purely logical ones. And since all other kinds of statement cannot, even in principle, be verified, then they are but pseudo-statements. Since scientific and empirical statements are about the phenomena of experience, then they give rise to generalizations and law-like statements which are predictive of further experiences in similar circumstances, however tentative these generalizations might be.

Furthermore, one can bring to bear upon them the precision afforded by mathematics. One can build up the quantitative base for trusting one set of claims over another. The systematic account of the world will seek to provide causal explanations.

One of the best 'philosophical translations' of positivism into educational theory, practice and research was provided by D. J. O'Connor in his book *An Introduction to the Philosophy of Education* (1956). O'Connor was highly critical of educational theory for its failure to give the clear verifiable statements which any theory required. In fact the theory was a mixture of value judgements, aims, and statements which were too loosely phrased for anyone to know what would count as evidence for or against them. There was a need to distinguish between the aims of education (the kind of statements which simply reflected one's emotional attachment) and empirically verifiable statements. These needed to be so stated that one would know what would verify or falsify them.

I do not want here to retail all the well-known and well-rehearsed criticisms of this philosophical position. Rather, I want to bring out the specific challenges it makes to educational research.

First, there can be no clear logical distinction between research into physical phenomena and research into social institutions and structures. Society can be studied scientifically. There are social facts, just as there are physical facts. People, despite their individuality, fall into types or groups, and general statements can be made about these types. Such generalizations can be verified. Gradually a theoretical picture can be built up which relates types to social structures, such that to explain why certain people act in the way they do one refers to the social structures which could be said to cause that kind of behaviour. Such social explanations contradict those which seek to explain behaviour in terms of personal choice or individual psychology. Of course, one cannot deny that there is some personal choice, but, first, such choice will be exercised within parameters determined by the social facts, and, second, *typical* behaviours are what are being explained – there can always be exceptions.

One of the 'founding fathers' of modern sociology, Emile Durkheim, took the chair of 'Science of Education' at the Sorbonne in 1902. For Durkheim, a proper science of society was essential for a more systematic study of educational policy and of teaching. Such a study could therefore serve pedagogy. That science of society treated institutions and social structures as facts – comprehensible only within the total educational system of which they were part.

To understand education, one needed to understand the function it had within the larger society. And that would differ from one society to another. Moreover, within any one social system different schools would serve different functions, whatever the rhetoric which claimed otherwise. This kind of functional analysis gave rise to a powerful research tradition within education, which is based on the principle that social structures determine the function of particular institutions and social understandings within society, and thus shape the expectations and understandings of individuals. This smacks of a certain causal determinism. We are what society has made us, and the process of so making us can be studied scientifically.

Second, the positivist spirit requires a clear distinction between the aims and values of education, on the one hand, and the means of reaching those ends, on the other. Matters of value are not open to empirical enquiry (and are thus outside the bounds of meaningful discussion) whereas the means of realizing those values are. Researchers are required to show how certain ends might be reached, not to say what those ends ought to be. A clear means/end distinction enters the politics of research and the management of education. Durkheim, for example, was interested to see practical results of his sociological studies; that is why he devoted so much time to lecturing to teachers and trainees. But he distinguished carefully between the job of social analysis and the moral interests which he hoped this social analysis would serve.

Implicit in what I have said are some of the major criticisms of positivism and thus of the kind of research which is inspired by it. First, the reduction of meaningful statements to those which explain things scientifically, or which express purely logical and mathematical relations, *either* omits as meaningless the distinctive ways in which we talk about persons *or* reduces them to statements about physical or social facts. Are we as persons not capable of transcending the social structures in which we find ourselves? And are these social facts not themselves created by the very human beings whom they are meant to explain? Second, the values are embedded within the social structures, beyond the control or responsibility of the individual. We cannot reason what these values should be – they are a matter of emotion, anyway, and to be explained causally as a function of the social needs.

One can see, therefore, the ferocity with which the positivist agenda and outlook came to be attacked. This was reflected in M. F. D. Young's edited book *Knowledge and Control* (1972) and

Filmer's *New Directions in Sociological Theory* (1972). They drew attention to the distinctively human way in which we make sense of the social world. That world cannot be studied as an object of science and observed as a thing in itself ('reified'). Rather is it *interpreted*, and to some extent a *construction* of those interpretations. This has massive implications for such standard research concepts as truth and verification, objectivity, reality and knowledge.

But before we consider these developments, we need to examine the features of positivism which cannot be rejected quite so easily.

First, a connection was made between the meaning of a statement and the way in which it is verified. One might argue that the logical positivists were wrong in their highly restricted list of how statements might be verified. Thus there is a need to include statements about other people and about social structures in a way that these are not logically reducible to statements about physical objects. But in so doing one is logically committed to there being distinctive ways of verifying such statements. Their truth or falsity depends on certain truth conditions, that is, conditions existing independently of my making the statement. When I say that someone told a lie, given what we mean by 'lie', then certain conditions prevailed, quite independently of me, which makes that a true or a mistaken claim. But those conditions are not the same as those which would make a statement about the physical world true or false. Therefore, nor would the mode of verification be the same. In rejecting what is thought to be positivism, many theorists wrongly reject, not just the narrow form of verification, but the very idea of verification itself.

Second, the recognition of a distinctively human capacity to engage in intentional and meaningful action should not distract us from the fact that, as Durkheim showed, there are social facts. These facts set the parameters of how we think. The values, which they embody, enter into the minds and intentions of the people within those societies. There are *types* of people, which reflect the social context in which these people find themselves. For example, the existence of an underclass has its sociological explanations, and membership of such a class will influence how its members think and aspire. There remains room for the kind of generalizations, however tentative, and causal explanations even within the interpretive traditions.

THE POLITICAL ARITHMETIC TRADITION

There is always a danger in labelling areas of research – of 're-ifying' it (as some sociologists would call it). But the danger of rejecting positivism wholesale is that one might well reject a tradition of educational research which has proved to be very fruitful indeed. 'Political arithmetic' is associated with a quantitative research tradition which requires the gathering of hard data, especially in relation to gender, ethnicity and social class, and of discovering the correlation of such data with subsequent performance and achievement. The assumption (indeed quite explicit assumption in some cases – see Heath, 2000, p. 314) is that one can legitimately speak of causal relations between, say, social class and academic performance, given the strength of correlations. Such a tradition, reflected in the work of Floud *et al.* (1956), Halsey *et al.* (1980), and Heath *et al.* (1990), provided the data for those who argued against selection into grammar schools. It claims to be 'atheoretical' and descriptive, letting the facts speak for themselves.

There is a danger that such a tradition might be undermined by those who, associating it with 'positivism' wholesale, reject this as a valid approach to educational research. And this danger is reflected in the decline inside departments of educational studies of people trained within the traditions of political arithmetic. In a nutshell, there is a shortage of good quantitative researchers.

Of course, in one sense, this is not 'atheoretical'. There is an assumption that 'facts speak for themselves', that descriptions, such as that of social class, can be attributed to people who are thus expected to behave in a distinctive and predictable way. The social class itself becomes a causal element in the chain of explanation of human achievement and performance.

In chapter 4, I have argued (against those who would reject the 'positivist' basis of educational research), that it is necessary to retain a notion of 'social fact' and indeed of 'causality' within an explanation of human, as well a physical, events. But I also argue that it is possible to do so without commitment to a thoroughly determinist position or to a rejection of the distinctively personal way in which the social world and experience is interpreted by each individual. It is the failure to see this which creates 'the false dualism' between quantitative and qualitative research (see p. 44).

On the other hand, there are (and will always be) difficulties over agreeing to such concepts or categories such as 'social class' or 'ethnic minority'. These are not classifications which 'stare you in the face'. They are ways of classifying which are parasitic upon a wider, cultural understanding of society – which understanding will shift as the economic basis of society changes and as critical examination of our concepts erodes previous ways of under-standing the social world. This does create problems in the longitudinal comparisons of 'social facts'.

INTERPRETIVE THEORY: INTENTIONS, SUBJECTIVITY AND PHENOMENOLOGY

The distinction is drawn between physical things and persons in that the latter, but not the former, interpret, or attach meaning to, themselves and others. To understand other people, therefore, requires understanding the interpretations which they give of what they are doing. We need to know their intentions. In chapter 4, I referred to this intentional aspect in our identification of an action as an action of a particular sort. What we do cannot be understood as observable behaviours alone. They are behaviours infused with intentions. The raising of my hand could be a signal for the revolution to take place, a gesture of welcome, or the seeking of attention. It all depends on what was intended.

From this follows a great deal about the explanation of people's behaviour. We need to know their intentions and their motives. We need to know how they understood or interpreted the situation. For this reason researchers talk of the *subjective meanings* of those whom they are researching – that is, the different understandings and interpretations which the participants bring with them to the situation. If one adds to that the belief that the social world is constituted by the intentions and meanings of the 'social actors', then there is nothing to study objectively speaking. To think otherwise would be to 'reify' (treat as objects independent of our thinking about them) what are in effect the creations of the social actors' own thinking and intentions. We each inhabit subjective worlds of meaning through which we interpret the social world. Indeed, that social world is nothing other than our interpretations.

That at least seems to be a popular view, and in the light of it researchers devote their time to revealing the interpretations of the situation by the social actors. This 'illuminates' what has happened. Otherwise we impose upon the situation interpretations which are not those of the participants and thus, *a fortiori*, not the ones through which the situation is to be understood.

None the less, one needs to be careful. Is it not possible for the social actor to *mis*interpret both her own and other people's actions? May it not be the case that someone else might give a better and truer account of my actions than me myself? We do talk of self-deception or of not understanding the whole picture. Others might see the ambition which the agent himself fails to recognize.

As must be clear, such an account creates a gulf between the kind of research within the positivist tradition and the research which stresses the intentionality of the social actors. But perhaps certain distinctions need to be made, reflecting different traditions of social explanation. Let us start with the phenomenology, which has had such a powerful influence.

The proponents of the new directions in sociology refer to Alfred Schutz and his seminal work, *The Phenomenology of the Social World*, in which he tried to lay the foundations of a phenomenological sociology. Schutz himself drew upon the phenomenology asso-ciated with the philosopher Edmund Husserl. It is difficult to capture in a few words what such a difficult philosopher said. But Husserl sought to provide an account of human consciousness which was free from any presuppositions. To do that required a special kind of inner reflection upon experience as it directly happened. Such experiences were 'intentional' in that they were experiences *of* something. But the nature of the experience was revealed by the subjective account of them, not by reference to an object existing independently of the experience of it. These 'objects', as experienced, were in the mind, and characterized by one's consciousness of them – their shape and colour, their relevance and significance, the causal links made with other objects, the ideas they conjured up and were associated with. These objects might be experienced as irritating, thought-provoking, threatening, pointing to future action. Certainly our experiences are selective, and the principle of selection is usually the relevance to perceived needs. Such modes of experiencing do not entail that that is how reality *objectively* is, as though independent of the experiencing itself. Similarly one represents others in this phenomenological way. It is not a matter of how they are in themselves. It is a matter of how they are experienced, how they are constructed by a person's subjective experience of them.

In his essay 'The Stranger', Schutz (1964) portrays the visitor to a strange society. What the stranger sees is imbued with his own preconceptions – with his own subjective interpretations. But he needs to understand how the practices of everyday life are constituted by the subjective meanings of the members of the society he has entered. Otherwise he will not survive. The everyday understandings of *his* society simply do not hold in the new one. Interpretations embedded in the practices of the new society do not tally with the preconceptions of the stranger, for they are created and maintained in existence only through the interpretations of those within the society who engage in these practices. Somehow the stranger needs to get on the inside, to share in those practices and be part of the society in its constant defining and redefining of reality. But even in entering that social world, so that world will be changed, for the stranger's negotiation of interpretations, as he tries to understand, becomes a further element in the construction of social reality. There is a constant interpretation, through which social reality is defined, and there arises an interpretation of those interpretations. Each person brings to those negotiations their own unique experiences and thus interpretations. Since no one can have had another person's life history, no one will share exactly the same interpretations and thus have the same experience.

The phenomenological emphasis upon the examination of experience as such, combined with the claim that such experience will be filtered through one's unique life experience, points to the importance of 'subjective meanings' or subjective interpretations of that experience in our understanding. One cannot get away from that subjective filtering of one's unique and personal experience, feeling and understanding. To understand particular events one must see things from the point of view of the participants or of the people who are involved – how they interpret events and thereby constitute those events as events of a certain sort. One might go further and seek to explain why people behaved in the way they did by trying to re-enact their life history, of which this particular action is part. Indeed, Collingwood (in his 1946 *The Idea of History* saw such imaginative re-enactment as essential to an under-standing of history.

There are, however, different ways in which 'interpretation' might be understood and in which it relates to the meaning to be attributed to what we do or say.

First, in asking for the meaning of what a person did, we do need to refer to the intentions which are embedded within the act. For example, an action is not just a physical movement. It is an intentional activity unintelligible without reference to those intentions. But even then there are various depths to one's possible analysis of 'intentional act'. 'The teacher intended to teach algebra.' 'The teacher intended to demonstrate his ability to teach Mary algebra.' 'The teacher intended to demonstrate his ability to teach Mary algebra from fear of otherwise being demoted.' So one might go on. Intentional explanations can refer simply to the conscious purpose of the act or to a wider explanatory scheme of things or to motives for so acting. 'Subjective meaning' therefore sometimes refers to the intentions which make the action intelligible – what the actor was thinking which is not open to immediate observation.

Second, the meaning of an action or of a situation refers to the wider significance of the action or situation for the agent. Thus the 'meaning' of Rome for me lies in the particular significance it has for my imagination or memory due to my having lived there in my youth. The 'subjective meaning' refers to the particular connotations and associations which Rome has for me but not for those who do not share my life history. Similarly with the meaning of 'school' or 'teacher', as it summons up a range of feeling and moods connected with particular incidents.

Third, the meaning of what I say, though associated with particular experiences and feelings that are mine and no one else's, employs words (and the grammar for putting those words together), which are 'public property'. Indeed, it is through learning how to use that language that I come to share in a range of public meanings through which I am able to organize my experience in a particular way and communicate it to other people. The meaning of the conclusions of a piece of educational research is, in one sense, the same for both writer and reader if they are both using the English language properly, even though, in another sense, that conclusion might mean something different if it conjures up quite different associations. But the subjective meanings of the latter do not entail subjective meanings of the former.

Fourth, the intentions which I have, embodied in actions or gestures or words, require an interpretation by someone else. Thus, the hand raised in salutation presupposes that this gesture will be interpreted in a particular way. This makes sense only if there is an understanding amongst a group of people of the rules, which give this behaviour that meaning. There are rules of everyday life, which make such meaningful encounters intelligible and thus possible. But such a requirement shows that our understandings are not constituted of 'subjective meanings', except in the trivial sense that the meaning of what is done is intelligible only by reference to the mental acts of the subject. But those mental acts refer necessarily to a language which embodies a publicly shared set of meanings and a socially shared set of rules through which relationships and communication are made possible. These are not the product of one's 'subjective meanings'.

Fifth, the meaning of an action or of an event or of a text refers to its significance which may be apparent to other people than the agent – and then only many years later. Mr Callaghan, when Prime Minister, could not have anticipated the interpretations of his speech at Ruskin College in 1976. Its meaning is understood within a cultural and educational framework which is still being interpreted in the light of further analysis. Thus great historical events are constantly open to revision; the 'full meaning' of the American Declaration of Independence was clearly not apparent to those who made the declaration. An understanding of the text of a Shakespeare play would not necessarily benefit from a declaration of intention from a reincarnated William – though that would be interesting.

Let me summarize this brief discussion of 'meaning' and 'interpretation'. If by 'subjective meanings' one means the feelings, personal connotations or associations that accompany a statement, gesture or action, then these are indeed subjective and private interpretations, and as such will no doubt limit the objectivity of what we do or say or believe. One can see, therefore, why researchers want to get at these in order to understand why people acted in the way that they did. (Think of the number of theses that simply chase the perceptions of the people being researched.) If, however, we mean by 'subjective meanings' the way in which a particular 'subject' or agent understands things, then the meanings are subjective only in a trivial sense. They are the understandings of this particular person or 'subject'. But such understandings, reflected in the intentions which inform a particular action or gesture or word, presuppose a public and thereby objective world of social rules and language through which their intentional behaviour makes sense. And as such these interpretations may be mistaken. Furthermore, an understanding of the meaning of what that person says or does is not reducible to how he or she sees it. They may be deceiving themselves. Or they may be working within a context of social and historical forces, which is beyond their comprehension.

However, it may still be argued that, although the rules which constitute social life and social facts (for example, the rules which make a relationship into a marriage) are inherited and not dependent on the subjective meanings of each individual, they are none the less socially constituted and their continued existence depends on social agreement. Such meanings change as people come to interpret things differently. Homosexual marriages would have been unintelligible a generation ago, but that is no longer the case. Agreement on interpreting things differently recreates social reality. If a neutron bomb or a nerve gas obliterated all human beings, then there would be no social facts – though physical reality would remain. That is because the social, but not physical, reality depends on the agreement of people to interpret things in this way. Similarly, the way in which we describe the motives of people depends upon the agreements within social groups of some taxonomy of possible motives. The list of virtues, for example, changes from culture to culture. Therefore, is not the way in which we interpret others, and indeed ourselves, socially constructed, and could not such interpretations have been otherwise?

The answer is both 'yes' and 'no'. Certainly, schools as organizations are defined in terms of the rules which everyone within those schools accepts – that certain kinds of knowledge are worthwhile and should be taught, that authority is to be respected, that performance should be assessed by explicit standards embodied within the examination system, and so on. And it is true that such rules (and thus the organization of the school) depend on the agreement of the different agents (parents, teachers, students) to them. The social reality of the school is maintained through such agreements. There are different kinds of schools in that they understand themselves differently in terms of agreed educational aims, beliefs about human nature and motivation, ideals of teacher/learner relationships. Hence, it would seem silly to subject Summerhill to the same criteria of success as a school conceived in a quite different way.

Again, the accounts that we give of such schools – in terms of the ambitions of the head teacher, the truculence of the students, the despondency of the teachers, the bureaucracy of the local education authority, the ominous threats of the inspectors – are dependent on interpretations of others' motives, attitudes, aspirations, intentions, values. Such accounts depend on the repertoire of explanatory descriptions at our disposal. And they could have been otherwise. Moreover, they may not be the ones which the head, the teachers, the students, the local authorities and the inspectors would have chosen. Hence, it seems doubly the case that social reality is a construction and that it reflects the subjective meanings of both the agents themselves and those who interpret what the agents do.

On the other hand, such 'social constructions', though maintained by social agreement, are an inherited feature of the world we are born into. They are embedded in the language which we acquire and through which we come to describe the social world and the relationships with each other. Any reconstruction of that social world must be a reconstruction of the 'given'. Moreover, the complex account that we give of that world requires distinctions which have to relate to a reality which is independent of my creative endeavours. The ambition of the head teacher or the truculence of the students is based on what are purported to be the intentional behaviours of each. Given what is meant by these terms, such accusations might simply be wrong. One cannot simply *choose* to create the head teacher as ambitious or the student as truculent.

Phenomenology focused upon the consciousness of the individual. Phenomenological research therefore aimed to uncover that subjective consciousness. It stressed the importance of the interpretation of events or of others' actions in the light of those 'subjective meanings'. 'Subjective meanings', however, could refer either to the associated ideas and feelings or to the intentions of the agent – and these too often get confused in the phenomenological account. It is further claimed that social reality is but a construct of such subjectivities. There is no social reality in the sense of something existing independently of them. The judgement that someone is acting from this or that motive is but a subjective interpretation of events.

But the proponents of such a view forget the implicit objectivity in what they are saying. The meaning of what they do or say depends on the existence of others who will interpret correctly what is said or done. There is a need for a shared language and set of social rules, through which those subjective understandings are formed and their intentions interpreted by others. Moreover, the distinctions made in the account we give of the social world, although they might be superseded by more useful distinctions, need a purchase on a real world, which makes those distinctions possible. The subjective meanings, except in the case of the third definition above, are parasitic upon acquaintance with an objective reality and not vice versa. To quote Bhaskar (1989), 'social practices are not exhausted by their conceptual aspect' (p. 4).

INTERPRETIVE THEORY: SOCIAL REALITY AND ETHNOGRAPHY

As I explained at the beginning, there are many ways in which one might map the different traditions in educational research and their philosophical underpinnings. The distinction which I draw between the phenomenological and ethnographic traditions is but one. But it reflects an interesting shift of emphasis, despite what is in common.

I have associated phenomenolgy with the emphasis upon the subjective meanings of the agent as these are revealed in the reflection upon the states of mind which inform their actions. This is rooted originally in the philosophy of Husserl. But it manifests itself in the rather careless reduction, by some educational researchers, of the meaning of what is said or done to the subjective states of mind of the agent. In some respects it is often useful to be aware of such states of mind. The truculence of the student may arise from an association of the lesson with memories which could not possibly have been anticipated by the teacher from the meaning of what was said. But, in confusing 'meaning' in the sense of the state of mind of the agent with 'meaning' in terms of the agreed rules of social behaviour and of language, the latter lose any objective reality. We enter a solipsistic world which makes even our gestures unintelligible. If one starts from the subjective meanings, there one will remain.

On the other hand, both gestures and the spoken word can be ambiguous. And that ambiguity leaves room for misinterpretation. Furthermore, the social reality is changed if those misinterpretations shape the relationships. Perhaps the teacher was not being sarcastic, but if that is how his words were perceived, then the relation between teacher and student changes. And that might be the most significant element in an understanding of what happened in the classroom.

Furthermore, as I have explained, the meaning of a gesture or statement does depend upon the social rules, whether or not embodied in language, through which those gestures or statements are to be interpreted. The command to be quiet has meaning only because of the agreed conventions which ensure that that is how it will be understood by the students. To understand any group, therefore, whether that be the wider society or whether it be the social groupings like the school within that society, requires a grasp of those social rules. Some of these are clear and obvious to anyone living in that society. Some are explicit, even backed by legal sanctions. Others are clearly part of the culture, as in the case of queuing at bus stops. But others are not so clear. They need to be discovered. Indeed, they may be so subtle that even those who subscribe to them in practice may not recognize them explicitly.

Teachers may not recognize the rules which give meaning to certain gestures, actions and words in the cultures of the students they teach. This can lead not only to obvious misunderstandings, but also to the teachers not grasping the dynamics of the classrooms they are in charge of. There is the danger, as in the case of Schutz's stranger, of interpreting the social rules and understandings which define and maintain social reality in this particular way, without reference to the interpretations given by those who meaningfully engage in the different activities. The stranger just does not understand.

There is, therefore, an important body of research which examines closely the reality of social situations like the 'everyday reality' of the school or the classroom (see, for example, Woods's *Divided School*, 1979, or Ball's *Beachside Comprehensive*, 1981, or Peshkin's *Growing Up American*, 1978) or of minority groups where the 'taken for granted meanings' of the dominant culture do not apply (see, for example, Mac an Ghaill's *Young, Gifted and Black: Student–Teacher Relations in the Schooling of Black Youth*, 1988). Such studies show how what happens in practice is not like the official account. Such studies, too, 'illuminate' the context in which teachers and others are working, making some policies and practices inappropriate and others more relevant. The official rhetoric of the educational programme might be that of broadening the mind or developing a critical perspective; the reality may be something different.

Ethnography, therefore, refers to that kind of research which takes seriously the perspectives and the interactions of the members of the social groups being studied. It is based on the premise that social reality cannot be understood except through the rules which structure the relations between members of the group and which make it possible for each to interpret the actions, gestures and words of the others. In this respect, it draws upon certain traditions within the social sciences, including that of anthropology. It aims to study the social world as it is, and that requires insight into that world through participation in it. Only then might one come to understand that reality. But this entails no relativism as so often is assumed. The social worlds being studied are as real and as objective as the physical world. They exist independently of the researcher.

There are, however, certain difficulties which need to be addressed.

First, does not the researcher, in participating in the social world or in the 'foreign culture' which is to be understood, thereby have to see that world or that culture in *its* terms, not in those of the researcher? In translating what has been learnt into their own terms for wider communication, researchers would no longer be talking about the social reality as that is defined by the participants. Is there not something logically odd about being both an insider and an outsider at the same time? For example, the researcher into the working-class youth culture of a notorious housing estate must let the youth speak for themselves in their 'natural setting'. Indeed, the research might simply leave it at that – an exposure of what is the case and no more. But that would not satisfy those who want to explain further the reasons or causes for what the young people do and say. Such further explanations arise from the need to improve the environment and safety of those who are not within that culture, or from the need to help the neighbourhood school function more effectively against that background. The reporting of the social understandings and beliefs which inform the relationships and behaviour of the youth, become the data for analysis and explanation. And that cannot be in the terms of those who are being researched into.

This issue is dealt with by Winch in his *The Idea of a Social Science* (1958) and later in his paper 'Understanding a Primitive Society' (1972). Winch was addressing the problem of how researchers can understand a society which is very different from their own – so different that there seems to be nothing recognizable in their social life. There is no understanding of their language. In no way do their actions seem intelligible. The social world of those being researched, constituted by very different understandings and social rules, could not be captured by the understandings of the researcher who inhabits a very different society.

Winch argues, however, that even in this extreme case there are certain common practices which enable the researcher to find some of the activities intelligible. There are activities concerned with obtaining and eating food, keeping warm, caring for the young and the elderly, legitimating certain kinds of relationships and not others, protecting from harm. That is, whatever the differences between societies and cultures, common elements are recognizable within a distinctively human form of life. *A fortiori*, that must be the case with regard to sub-cultures within one's own society. To understand the meaning attributed to certain actions, gestures and speech acts by a distinctive cultural group (for example, by an ethnic minority group or by a religious sect) requires an understanding of these from their point of view. But given certain facts about human beings – the desire to meet certain biological needs, the typical human emotions of fear, loyalty, ambition, etc. – then what makes their actions intelligible to them makes those same actions potentially intelligible to the outsider. Having grasped the significance of particular rituals within Winch's primitive society, howsoever different they may be from what the researcher has previously experienced, they become intelligible in terms of an explanatory framework which could be applied within the researcher's own society. I say 'could be applied', because the researcher's society, as Winch points out, may be dominated by explanatory frameworks which, by themselves, would not make the actions of another society intelligible. For instance, the assumption that an action is intelligible only in an instrumental sense – as a means to an end – may lead to a misunderstanding of the actions that the researcher is seeking to explain. But other forms of explanation are available to the researcher – actions as expressions of emotion, gestures as signs of respect, stories as sense-making myths – which could be applied to the society being studied. There is no reason why therefore the explanations which the researcher wishes to give, though not ultimately in the terms used by those being researched, should not relate to them, thereby making the group's activities intelligible to those who are not members of that group. As Winch argued,

> Although the reflective student of society, or a particular mode of social life, may find it necessary to use concepts which are not taken from the forms of activity which he is examining, but which are taken from the context of his own investigation, still these technical concepts of his will imply a previous under-standing of those other concepts which belong to the activities under investigation. (1958, p. 89)

The second kind of difficulty is not unrelated. Even if the social rules of the group being researched into can be grasped by the outsider (and thus their activities made intelligible) what is being understood will necessarily be unique. The social reality under investigation is not the same as other social realities since each is constituted by the distinctive interactions, perceptions and inter-pretations of the members of the social group. Each group will be defined in terms of its own negotiated meanings. What can be said of one group cannot be applied to another. This would seem to leave educational research a fairly parochial matter, for each social setting, to be understood, would require its own ethnographic study. One could not transfer the conclusions from one study to an understanding of other social settings, because each social setting is defined by the perceptions and interactions of those who are participating in that particular social reality.

Such a view would seem to support the criticism of those who complain about the non-cumulative nature of educational research. Lots of unique studies, however interesting and cleverly carried out, seem to add up to nothing. No generalizations can be drawn from them and therefore they do not help those who make policy or who engage in professional practice in social settings which so far have not benefited from ethnographic studies.

This criticism, however, rests on the 'uniqueness fallacy'. The 'uniqueness fallacy' is to argue from the fact that everyone or every group is unique in some respect to the claim that everyone and every group is unique in every respect. Thus I am unique in that only I occupy this particular space at this particular time and only I have my life history. But I am not unique in being an Englishman, or working at Oxford University, or being married with three daughters. We are all unique in some respects and not in others. The objects of the ethnographic studies are in one sense unique, thereby discouraging too hasty a generalization from them. In many other ways they are not unique; the members of the groups under examination share with other human beings certain typical emotions and feelings, aspirations and hopes, needs and wants. In pointing to uniqueness we must not forget what is typical of people in that kind of situation. That is why those who recognize the uniqueness of an ethnographic study do none the less find it 'illuminating'. They recognize what is in common with *similar* situations. And it is surely an aim of research to identify the relevant similarities.

The importance of this becomes urgent as there is a shift towards the systematic reviews of research along the Cochrane model in evidence-based health care. That model is focused on large-scale randomized controlled tests with carefully observed interventions – a model of research firmly within the positivist framework. The unjustified emphasis upon the uniqueness of ethnographic studies will exclude these from such systematic reviews, whatever the insights and 'illuminations' they bring. Failure to recognize the fallacy of uniqueness will impoverish the evidence-based research to be conducted for the benefit of policy and practice.

The third difficulty to be faced by ethnographic researchers is the claim that the participation by the researcher in the social interactions of the group necessarily changes that situation to something else. The research activity changes that which is being researched into. The very questions and statements of the researcher alter the perceptions and thus the definition of the social situation by the members of the group.

The impact of the researcher is not to be denied. The conclusions of the research cannot be about the situation as it was originally to be investigated. There is not the objectivity in the sense of an observer recording what is the case, insulated from that which is being researched into. But one can exaggerate the problems. The social setting being investigated, if well established, is rooted in traditions which are not to be easily shifted by a stranger in the midst. The social roles and understandings will have been too deeply internalized. The impact of the researcher could be significant in smaller, more ephemeral social settings – like the classroom. But even there it *need* not be if the researcher takes the right precautions. One needs to reflect again upon the nature of social reality. Though constituted and maintained by the inter-pretations and agreements of the participants, changing that reality is more like rebuilding a ship at sea than it is like exchanging a bit of furniture. One can agree to do the latter and complete the task swiftly. One is unlikely to be sitting on the furniture to be exchanged. But the former requires the very careful, bit by bit approach resulting in a vessel which is partly formed in accordance with that from which it has developed. Talk about each person's construction of reality often appears as if it is a matter of exchanging furniture. One *chooses* to construct things in one way rather than another. But this is quite clearly incoherent.

A 'practice' is, as I explained in chapter 2, 'a collection of different activities that are united in some common purpose, embody certain values and make each of the component activities intelligible'. An *educational practice* is one where the set of activities is united in the purpose of getting people to learn – and to learn what is thought by the educator and the educational system to be of value. To understand any one educational practice is to understand how the actors interpret such a broad agenda. One can imagine different ways in which the transaction between teacher and student is interpreted. The teacher, embracing a child-centred philosophy of education, would try to set the rules of interaction in a way which took seriously the perceptions and interests of the learner. The students, coming with their own agendas, would contribute their understanding of the relationship which the teacher is trying to establish. And that contribution will be influenced by the students' previous experience of teachers. Such transactions, however, will take place, more often than not, within a wider social set of understandings of what education is for and how it should be conducted. To understand an educational practice would be to grasp these interacting understandings, beliefs and values. There is a clear difference between a practice where the teacher is pursuing ideals about the intrinsic worth of the subject being taught and the teacher who sees its value in purely utilitarian terms. Not only are different values embodied in the practice, but also different criteria for selecting content and teaching method. For example, an organized discussion of controversial issues is to be understood in terms of the intentions and values which lie behind the selection of this approach and the way in which it is interpreted. The Humanities Curriculum Project embodied a distinctive educational practice, albeit research would need to examine how this was interpreted in different instances of it. In this regard one should note the way in which the evaluation of that project gave rise to a research tradition in which ethnographic studies were accepted as essential.

These considerations show the inappropriateness of the kind of research, within the positivist framework and spirit, which treats 'discussion groups' or 'the teaching of controversial issues' or 'size of group' or 'reference to textual evidence in the discussion' as hard data for empirical enquiry and the establishment of general, verifiable principles. Such practices can be understood only in the light of how the teachers and the learners perceive what they are doing. In the case of the Humanities Curriculum Project, such perceptions were informed by an agreed set of values and procedures which the teachers and their students learnt and internalized, although inevitably with some variations. None the less, from case studies of particular practices, a picture could be constructed about the appropriate conditions and training and people for such an educational practice to be undertaken.

THE POSTMODERN EMBRACE

A challenge to the kind of research, which its critics would like it to be, comes from the 'postmodern embrace'. The person most closely associated with this would be Jean-Francois Lyotard, whose book,

The Postmodern Condition: a Report on Knowledge (1984), has had such a profound influence. Briefly, the book reflected upon major changes in society and the impact that such changes had and will continue to have upon what counts as knowledge and how it should be treated. The implications for education – for what counts as an educational practice and for how such practices should be understood and organized – are immense. At one level, the book might be seen as pointing to the breakdown of consensus in today's pluralist and multicultural society and to the implications of this. But at a more profound level, it invites us to question what counts as knowledge and truth, and what sense can be attached to verifying what is claimed to be true.

It makes sense, in understanding what is meant by *post*modernism, to reflect on what it is being contrasted with, namely, 'modernism'. 'Modernism' refers to a long and dominant cultural tradition, which has the following characteristics:

First, as is reflected in the positivist tradition outlined in chapter 4, there is the ideal of a complete and scientific explanation of physical and social reality. Though this might not in practice be possible, it remains an intelligible ideal.

Second, in pursuit of this ideal, the progressive development of knowledge can be divided into its intellectual disciplines, based on their distinctive concepts, verification procedures and modes of enquiry. Through such diverse and disciplined study and research, bodies of knowledge are built up from indisputable premises.

Third, these bodies of knowledge provide the secure knowledge-base for social action and improvement.

Fourth, there is thus a 'grand narrative' which we have subscribed to, namely, the 'enlightenment' view that reason, in the light of systematically researched evidence, will provide the solutions to the various problems we are confronted with.

Fifth, the educational system is crucial to the initiation of young people into these different bodies of knowledge and forms of rationality. This is achieved by teachers who, through their education and training, have become 'authorities' within these different forms of knowledge.

What typifies the postmodern world is a questioning of each of these premises. Thus we live in a culturally diverse society which makes us question the dominance of any one view of the world. There are different perspectives and what counts as reasonable is defined differently within each perspective. By different perspectives I mean a variety of different viewpoints – feminist, ethnic minority, religious, and so on – which were previously ignored as though they were of no significance in our account of the world. Just as Kuhn argued in *The Structure of Scientific Revolutions* (1970) that scientific rationality was defined within a particular paradigm and that, therefore, the shift from one paradigm to another could not itself be a matter of scientific rationality, so too with rationality more generally within the postmodern world. Rival disputes about what is to count as a rational view of the world cannot be settled by appeal to reason. There is no 'meta-narrative' of rationality to which we can appeal and which will bring a certain unity to this diversity.

As a consequence there is a blurring of the boundaries between intellectual disciplines or subjects such that the self-contained nature of these subjects is questioned – both logically and organizationally. There is a questioning of whether the perspectives, which traditionally have been included within them, are the only perspectives. New subjects vie with the old ones for a place on the curriculum – women's studies, black studies, media studies, popular culture, and many more. There is no grand narrative which legitimates one set of values rather than another or one way of organizing knowledge rather than another. Therefore, we need to come to terms with pluralism, not simply in recognizing that there is a diversity of culture, but also in recognizing the diverse modes of rationality and of perspective. Is not reason, too, a social construct?

Furthermore, if reason itself is a social construct (and there are many constructions of it) then certain consequences follow. First, what counts as rational depends on the agreement between people, and that agreement is reached through 'negotiation'. But, as we all know, negotiations can be skewed according to who wields most power. The shape of knowledge – the acceptable statements within it, the modes of verifying what is true, the valid modes of enquiry – are legitimated more often than not by those who are in positions to define what counts as knowledge. One has in mind the university professors, the editors of journals who decide what is to be published, the publishers and reviewers of books. Knowledge and rationality are controlled by those who are in positions of power. If, for example, they are men, then a feminist perspective will be neglected. Postmodernism, therefore, is characterized culturally and intellectually by a revolt against this control and by an assertion of different modes of cultural expression. And, of course, the revolutionary developments in communications technology enable this to happen. It frees people from the restrictive practices which were pursued under the title of rationality. Educational debate – research and scholarship and argument – is as diverse in its outlets as it is in its appeal to legitimacy. And who, on this view, has any right to censor it?

A second consequence is the severance of the link between knowledge and certainty. It was part of the 'enlightenment project' to build, bit by bit, from basic and certain foundations, and by thorough verification of the interim conclusions, bodies of knowledge in which we could have complete confidence. But recognition, first, of the diversity of perspectives, second, of the theory-laden or perspective-influenced nature of basic observations, and, third, of the competing modes of rational procedure from premises to conclusion, undermines this sense of certainty. We live by hope, not by faith, and with very little charity.

'Foundationalism' seemed central to the 'enlightenment project', because if uncertainty existed in the premises of the search for knowledge then the whole structure would be unsound. Therefore, Descartes, in his *Discourse on the Method of Rightly Directing One's Reason and of Seeking Truth in the Sciences* (1637), tried through the systematic doubt of his beliefs to arrive at what simply could not be doubted. Such self-evidently true propositions would provide the certain foundation upon which to build a body of knowledge. But with the failure of such an enterprise we are left with what Wittgenstein referred to as a variety of language games, each with its own rule of discourse. There is no higher language game for instilling order into the variety.

The consequences for education of this postmodern critique are far reaching. First, there is a questioning of the authority-based organization and delivery of 'knowledge', as though this is a 'given' legitimated by agreed rational procedures. Once this assumption is doubted, then the authority of educational establishments and their representatives is undermined. The authoritative exposition gives way to a transaction between teacher and pupil; 'conversation' and 'negotiation' are more appropriate metaphors than 'initiation' and 'instruction'. Second, the organization of teaching into traditional subjects is questioned. Are not the areas of intellectual and cultural interest outside or across these subject boundaries – media, environmental, cultural, feminist or European studies, for example? And there is a growing disconnection between the subject organization of higher education and that of schools, as higher education increasingly accepts the challenge to the hegemony of traditional ways of organizing knowledge. Third, the location of knowledge (its maintenance and transmission) in schools, colleges and universities, dedicated to that purpose, seems to many to be increasingly questioned. Communications technology opens up other avenues for engaging with others in the pursuit of knowledge. Other 'stakeholders' (businesses, public services, educational entrepreneurs without accreditation) provide alternative venues for learning and research. There is, therefore, a gradual undermining of the institutional creation and distribution of knowledge as we have known it. Fourth, there is a resistance to the one 'grand narrative' which is attempting to replace that of the 'enlightenment', namely, that which Lyotard refers to as 'performativity'.

It is argued by Lyotard that the place of one 'grand narrative', as it is subverted by the spirit of postmodernism, is simply being replaced by another. We may have lost confidence in the dream of the enlightenment – the growth of knowledge, which is of value in itself. But we have replaced it with another kind of knowledge – that which serves economic growth and prosperity. Hence, the penetration of educational language by the new language of 'performativity', which I referred to in chapter 2. It tries to become the 'grand narrative', penetrating the different forms of discourse. The dominant values which legitimate what is taught are concerned with effectiveness in achieving useful ends, not about the 'transcendental virtues' of truth, beauty and goodness. Hence, it drives out these other forms of discourse about education as being of no significance.

I have much sympathy with this postmodern analysis. The cultural diversity which we now experience calls into question many of the certainties which previously were taken for granted. It points to the genesis and organization of knowledge as at least in part contingent upon social factors and exercise of control by those in powerful positions. It raises critical questions about the mode of learning (the transmission of knowledge) encouraged by the certainties of modernism. It points to the absence of the perspectives of those without a power base from which to teach. But some of the philosophical conclusions drawn from this cultural analysis seem to be mistaken.

This was illustrated in the much acclaimed book by Stronach and MacLure: *Educational Research Undone: the post-modern embrace* (1997). The general theme of the book was that so much educational research has been, and remains, faulty because it is unenlightened by the insights of postmodernism, and resistant to its embrace. Such insights were essentially philosophical in their questioning of assumptions about the nature and organization of knowledge, the objectivity of what is said in different fields of discourse, the foundation of our knowledge claims and the verification of them. In effect, Stronach and MacLure engage in what might be referred to as 'descriptive metaphysics' – defining the central concepts through which we understand our capacity to think about experience. Concepts which (under the influence of modernism) were previously thought to be indispensable, such as 'reason' and 'truth', become dispensable. There is a neglect of distinctions between truth conditions and verification, between knowledge and certainty, between interpretation of reality and reality itself, between text and the understanding of text, between reasons and proof.

But such a blurring of these distinctions is not entailed by the postmodern insights. The pursuit of truth makes sense without the guarantee of ever having attained it. The belief in rationality is compatible with the provisional and fallible nature of one's conclusions. The acceptance of a reality independent of the researcher does not contradict the possibility of many interpretations of that reality. As Carr (1997) pointed out in his inaugural lecture 'Professing Education in a Postmodern Age', a central tradition in philosophy has been to question received arguments and to seek the truth whilst knowing that the conclusions would always remain provisional, to respect those texts which encapsulate a well-argued position without regarding them as beyond criticism or improvement, to respect the giving of reasons whilst recognizing that the canons of good reasoning might evolve though criticism or vary according to type of discourse. Living with uncertainty is not the offshoot of postmodernism. It is the essence of the perennial philosophical tradition.

CONCLUSION: KNOWLEDGE, FALLIBILITY AND THE POLITICS OF EDUCATIONAL RESEARCH

'Dualisms', as Dewey called them, can be deceptive. Just as the sharp contrast between quantitative and qualitative research misleads us, so too does the contrast between the modern and the postmodern. The attack on 'foundationalism' came most effectively from Karl Popper who had been a member of the Vienna Circle and who would not normally appear in the hagiography of postmodernism. Popper, in *The Logic of Scientific Discovery* (1959), proposed 'falsifiability' rather than 'verifiability' as a criterion of meaning – and then only of the meaning of scientific statements and theories. Any theory is always open to revision in the light of further experience and criticism. We can never be certain that our beliefs and theories are correct. But we can feel confident in them if they have been subjected to the most rigorous testing.

To call his book the logic of scientific *discovery* had a certain irony to it. Discovery comes in all sorts of ways, without much respect for logic. Indeed, there may well be a sociological story to tell about how it came about. But Popper was concerned not with the provenance of scientific knowledge but with its status. Basically, one should believe only that which has been thoroughly corroborated through further experiments and through critical examination by others. In this way one can build up bodies of knowledge, however tentative these may be. What is important is that they have survived critical scrutiny. They are constantly put to the test. They contain the best theories that we have, in that they explain a lot, they do a better explanatory job than rival theories and they have survived criticism.

Of course, the development and the maintenance of knowledge requires institutional support (for example, the provision of libraries, publications, forums for critical debate) and there is no reason to deny the possibility of corruption here as elsewhere in public life. There will always be those who try to exercise their power to control or prevent criticism, or to promote certain opinions at the expense of others. The sociology of knowledge-creation demonstrates that fact (see, for example, Toulmin, 1972).

However, a story about the provenance of knowledge has little to do with the status or validity of the knowledge claims. The sociological story of the growth and organization of knowledge is not the same as, and cannot be a substitute for, the philosophical analysis and justification of that knowledge. Certainly, we organize knowledge in different subjects; there is a story to be told about how this organization came about; other ways of organizing knowledge are possible; there are bloody stories about the maintenance of some disciplines at the expense of others – and certainly lots of foul play. But the very distinction between foul and fair play, between mistaken and correct organizations of knowledge, presupposes that the analysis and critique of the organization and content of knowledge is not a matter for social science alone. There are facts about reality which constrain what can be said. One cannot avoid the common sense framework through which experience must be organized (*objects* existing in space and time, *causal relations* between objects, *persons* explained in terms of intentions and motives, *social settings* of rule-governed behaviour, *shared meanings* of communicating communities, *values* in terms of which choices are made). And the traditions through which these basic facts about reality have come to be conceptualized, tested out and found adequate, are 'givens' which evolve through criticism and discovery, not through the fiat of those in positions of power. Such bodies of knowledge remain tentative and provisional. They are always being tested out against further experience and criticism. Today's wisdom might be tomorrow's folly unless one is alert to circumstances which cast doubt on that wisdom.

This in general terms seems equally applicable to both the physical and the social worlds. But differences are pointed out which cast doubt on whether there can be an accumulation of knowledge of the social world as there can be of the physical world. *A fortiori*, there can be no such accumulated knowledge to inform educational practice. The critics of educational research refer to standards which are not applicable.

The reasons for those doubts have been rehearsed in the previous pages. Briefly, they arise from the peculiar nature of social reality and thus of our knowledge of it. That reality is constituted and maintained by the agreements in interpretation of the members of the society and of the groups within it. Moreover, those agreements – the 'meanings' which they attribute to words, gestures and actions – are evolving and will change as the understandings of the actors within the social setting change. Hence, there is something unique to each society and group, a different 'social construction'. The transaction between one teacher and her class in one school will be significantly different from transactions in other classes and in other schools. Superficially they may look the same. But the meanings attributed to the transactions by the participants, with their own distinctive life stories, are sufficiently different to make generalization impossible. That at least is how the story goes. Research, therefore, of the ethnographic kind, uncovers the uniqueness of each social setting. It is critical of that research which ignores this uniqueness in its search for general truths. The educational practice to be researched into belies the possibility of a science of teaching.

I have argued against such an extreme position for the following reasons. There is a social reality – social facts – which exists independently of this or that individual and which determines in some measure how people see and understand the world. In learning a language, or in coming to understand and work within the customs of the society, so people are both empowered and constrained by the social reality they find themselves in. In that sense, one might talk of social as well as physical causes. Furthermore, one might develop a theoretical perspective on, or a body of knowledge about, the links, say, between poverty and educational achievement, or between family relations and the propensity to commit crime.

However, such theoretical perspectives will constantly need to be refined in the light of more detailed studies. They will need to adapt to the changing social context which affects the nature of the connections. For example, the very different social conditions of the twenty-first century doubtless affect the connections between poverty and social achievement. And that difference will arise in part from the significance attached to poverty by the impoverished people themselves. Hence, theoretical perspectives concerned with social reality need to be more tentative, more ready to cope with the exception, more adaptable to the changing consciousness of those who are part of that reality.

The refining of the generalizations comes from the more detailed studies of the different social realities – the complex sets of rules through which actions are intended and interpreted, the impact of the social context upon the understandings of the social actors, the beliefs and moral perspectives of the participants. But the uniqueness of each context does not entail uniqueness in every respect. There are similarities between different social contexts as each is part of a wider society in which certain understandings and customs prevail. The individual members of these different groups have common fears, desires, aspirations and weaknesses. One can exaggerate the differences between people and how their behaviour might be explained.

An educational practice is informed by a set of aims and by an agreed set of procedures. It is imbued with values which structure the relationship between teacher and learner, and between these, on the one hand, and a tradition of what is worth learning, on the other. Learning to teach is as much a matter of being initiated into the values and understandings of that practice as it is of learning skills of classroom management or of marking books. The engagement in that practice requires both the recognition of the uniqueness of the transactions which it represents and also the commonality between that and other practices which share the same perspectives and values. For that reason, the teachers are able to draw upon the more general bodies of knowledge which inform that practice. Tentative they may be, but if they have been well researched they are the best we have.

However, due to the changing nature of educational practice – different situations, shifting values, changing educational aims, impact of policy – there needs always to be a sceptical and questioning stance towards theory. It is there to inform the professional judgement of the teacher. Research, which purports to provide answers to how one should perform, must necessarily be treated with caution. It needs, certainly, to be taken into account in the deliberations of the teacher. But it is but one element in those deliberations. No research can dictate to this teacher in this situation exactly how he or she should teach.

Such deliberation, however, requires a context in which the teacher might exercise that judgement. If there is knowledge without certainty, then that knowledge must always be open to critical scrutiny. There need to be the forums in which research is subject to scrutiny, in which educational practices can be questioned, and in which generalizations might be tested against the professional judgement and the experience of the teacher. Perhaps that suggests a greater role for the teacher in educational research, which is what will be considered in the next chapter. But more important for the conclusion of this chapter is the reminder of the tentativeness of knowledge and research, and the importance, therefore, of institutionalizing the possibility of criticism. As Popper argued, there cannot be growth of knowledge without criticism. There is no other way of eliminating error. But that goes against the grain as far as politicians are concerned.

Research into practice: action research and practitioner research

TEACHER AS RESEARCHER

An educational practice consists of a range of transactions between teachers and learners. Such transactions are *educational* because they are guided by certain aims and values. The aim is that the students should learn. The values relate to the manner in which those transactions take place and to the worth of that which is to be learnt.

Educational research, therefore, must be centrally, though by no means exclusively, focused on those transactions – on the ways in which learning is encouraged, nurtured, planned and brought about, and on the values which are embedded within them. Such transactions are complicated indeed. The teacher is constantly adjusting to unforeseen circumstances, responding to the levels of understanding of the learners, trying new approaches. The teacher is managing a situation which is fluid, unpredictable, dynamic. And this must be the case, for, as we said in chapter 4, there can be no straightforward causal connection between the teacher's intervention and the learning outcomes. There are too many interacting elements, including the beliefs and understandings of the learner through which the teacher's actions are interpreted.

The first thing to note, therefore, is the sheer complexity of these transactions – of the values and aims which inform the educational practice, of the constant adjustments of the teacher, and of the beliefs and interpretations of the learner. And all these must be seen within the physical and social constraints which are peculiar to this or that school, classroom or transaction. Given this complexity, it is difficult to see how the 'outside' researcher, from brief acquaintance or periodic visit, can understand it. Data gathered on one visit would not be the same as data gathered on a later visit. The critical incident on Thursday would not be the same as that on Friday, whatever the superficial resemblance. And in any case, that incident cannot be understood without reference to the social rules which teachers and taught subscribe to and which enable life to continue relatively smoothly. Nor can it be understood without reference to the intentions of the teacher and the beliefs of the learner.

For that reason, Stenhouse (1975) argued for the teachers to be, not the objects of research by the 'outsider', but the researchers themselves. Only they, on a daily basis, have access to the data crucial for an understanding of the classroom. And this is a philosophical as much as a practical point. An understanding of the situation requires reference to the accepted social rules and values within which the teachers are operating. It requires, too, reference to the teachers' interpretation of these rules and to the constant, often minute, judgements by which teachers adapt to evolving situations, interpret the learners' responses and make the guiding values concrete. Only teachers can have access to judgements of that kind. But, more than that, the tentative beliefs or conclusions drawn by the teacher become 'hypotheses' to be put to the test in the classrooms. Only the teachers can do that.

This emphasis upon the privileged position of the teacher in relation to the essential data of research raises questions about the nature of educational research and about the validity of much of it. And it is necessary to see how far the pursuit of these questions forces us to set limits to the possibilities within, and the value of, 'teacher researcher'.

First, it challenges the appropriateness of the kind of research which ignores the teacher's and learner's perspectives, the data which only the teacher can get access to, and the active testing by the teacher of the applicability in the classroom of either the research conclusions or the curriculum prescriptions.

Second, it sheds doubt on the endeavour to create a science of teaching, a definitive and proven account of how each and every teacher should teach. Those who make such a claim ignore the relevance and diversity of the 'logic of the subject matter' (see chapter 2), the variability of social reality (see chapter 4), the unpredictability of interacting elements (see chapter 5), and the differences of value, perception and educational aims which teachers bring to the classroom (see chapter 5). Deliberation and judgement in the light of evidence, critical reflection in the light of observation and analysis, reappraisal in the light of discussion and advice are more appropriate than the application to particular cases of general principles. And, if this is the case, then classrooms should be seen as laboratories in which the teacher, with a view to improving the learning of the students, is constantly testing out the ideas, the methods, the values which he or she brings to the transaction. Indeed, John Dewey established such a 'laboratory school' for testing out his educational ideas when he moved to Chicago in 1894 as Professor of Pedagogy. The good teacher is, through reflecting on the evidence, ever ready to adapt the ways in which those transactions are conducted. Moreover, the school – the community of teachers and learners – would also be seen as a community where this more research-based approach to teaching would be acceptable and nurtured. Such a place would accept failure as an opportunity for improving teaching and for formulating new approaches. Knowledge grows through the encouragement of criticism, not through its suppression.

Third, however, this elevation of the teacher to the status of researcher would seem to demote the significance of the large-scale studies, the general connections made between social structures and educational performance, or the links established between social and economic conditions and low standards. Theory, as the guide to professional practice advocated by O'Connor (see above, page 93), would have little or no place.

Fourth, however, acknowledgement of this privileged position of the teacher in educational research raises questions about the objectivity and impartiality of the researcher. Objectivity suggests that the researcher should be somewhat distant from what is being researched into. Prejudice, self-interest, familiarity, defensiveness would surely distort the research of the teacher. Who is likely to seek to falsify the very principles on which his teaching is based?

Finally, does not research require a theoretical perspective, a set of interrelated beliefs, which pick out some data as important and not others and which highlight certain features as important rather than others? And need teachers, intelligently engaged in the complexity of educational practice, have *theories* about what they are doing? If teachers are to be considered as researchers, then (one would seem entitled to ask) from what theoretical position are the teachers selecting certain data rather than other, or giving that interpretation of the data rather than an alternative one?

There are various answers to these questions, which help us refine the notion of the teacher as a researcher, and they are best approached through a brief examination of a tradition of curriculum research and evaluation which is closely associated with Stenhouse but which has been developed explicitly by Elliott (1991). The curriculum issues which Stenhouse addressed, at the time when in Britain the school-leaving age was being raised to 16, concerned the provision of an educational experience for young people who would normally have left school at 15 and whom many thought were more suited to practical and vocational education and training. For Stenhouse, however, these young people were as much in need of, and were as much capable of benefiting from, access to the humanities as those who had been assessed as academically superior. What was required was a reassessment of the curriculum, especially the pedagogy which must be considered as part and parcel of the curriculum. And that reassessment required, too, an examination of the aims of, and the values in, the teaching of the humanities, the way in which the humanities might inform the judgements of the students in their practical living, the selection of material to support that teaching, the teaching styles to be adopted, and the rights of the students to have their views protected. No simple prescription or formula would do. Teachers were expected not just to teach the humanities; they were explorers in new and unknown territory.

Indeed, Stenhouse defined the curriculum in research terms: 'A curriculum is an attempt to communicate the essential principles and features of an educational proposal in such a form that it is open to critical scrutiny and capable of effective translation into practice' (Stenhouse, 1975, p. 4). The problem that Stenhouse saw in so many educational proposals was that they were set out as a set of intentions, untested and never subject to critical scrutiny. It was as though those who prescribed the curriculum (for example, the government), distant from the transactions within each classroom, knew best and that the translation of those prescriptions into practice was relatively unproblematic. The gap between intention and reality was rarely explored. To explore it required asking what would happen if. . ., that is, hypothesizing the effects of implementing the intentions which underpinned the curriculum. Such an exploration would necessarily require an examination of pedagogy, resources, context, values, even the relevance of the wider government framework. Moreover, such an exploration would inevitably reflect back upon the assumptions and values of the original intentions. The very act of implementing them might create a new and unintended situation affecting the social world in which the 'curriculum' was to be implemented. Thus Putnam and Borko

(2000) refer to 'situated cognition' (and indeed 'situative theorists'!). They argue that: 'The physical and social contexts in which an activity takes place are an integral part of the activity, and the activity is an integral part of the learning that takes place within it' (p. 4).

By way of illustration, the 'Stenhouse curriculum experiment' was this. The humanities were those studies concerned with the distinctively human questions about practical living. These questions concerned such issues as relations between the sexes, the existence and tolerance of poverty, the use of violence to pursue social and individual goals, the conditions of a just war, the relationship to various forms of authority including parents, racial and ethnic relations. Such areas of practical living were essentially controversial. By that was meant that they involved matters of value about which there was no consensus in our society. Being controversial in this sense, the teacher had no authority to say what was the right answer to specific questions. Rather must the answers be thought, argued and deliberated about in the light of appropriate evidence. Such evidence was to be found in literature, poetry, history, theology, the arts, the sciences. Hence, the curriculum consisted of a lot of proposals concerning the use of such evidence in the deliberations about areas of practical living which divided society. The students, as indeed their parents and teachers, could not avoid such issues. How then might such issues be handled in the classroom?

To answer such a research question it was necessary to formulate certain hypotheses concerning the use of evidence, the involvement of the students in deliberation, the encouragement of reflective thinking, the role of the teacher, the protection of minority views. And these hypotheses needed to be tested out in the context of each classroom. Certain hypotheses were well confirmed in the practice of the teachers; the confirmation of others depended on context, ethos of the school, or personality of the teacher. The curriculum, therefore, was more than a set of written intentions. It was a set of tentative prescriptions about how learning might take place and how certain values might be made concrete in the teaching. Those values, in turn, reflected beliefs about the nature of knowledge, about the aim of education and about the value of curriculum content and procedures. Indeed, the curriculum was seen as an enormous, albeit daily, research project in which the teachers were, and had to be, the principal researchers.

As Elliott (1991) points out, there was always a danger of the teachers being considered as the mere collectors of other people's data. And in the subsequent Ford Teaching Project, therefore, the teachers were more active in formulating the hypotheses, in putting them to the test, and in clarifying the values which underpinned this work. They formed active networks of teacher researchers – forums for critiquing practice. The relationship between theory and practice shifted from that in which practice is seen to be an application of theory to one in which reflection upon practice reveals the theory embedded within it – and thus open to theorizing. This seems a crucial shift in perspective if we are to understand defensible programmes of educational research.

For example, the 'literacy hour', which is now a requirement in British primary schools and which sets out in detail the content and processes for teaching literacy, should on this view be regarded as a set of hypotheses rather than as a prescription. It needs to be constantly tested in terms of teaching styles, pedagogical practices, resources, school policy and effects upon the rest of the curriculum. Then one gradually refines the policy and practice through critical scrutiny of them as a result of experiencing them in action. Furthermore, the curriculum should thus be seen as a set of proposals which is constantly being implemented, tested out, found wanting in some respect, leading to the formulation of fresh proposals. As Stenhouse said, referring to Popper, 'improvement is possible if we are secure enough to face and study our failures'. Only teachers were in a position to put the hypotheses to the test.

THEORY AND PRACTICE

By contrast with what was said above, in which the teachers were invited to theorize about the curriculum and to formulate effective and appropriate procedures, it has often been thought that, through research, one might build up a theory of worthwhile and effective practice. Practice would follow from that theory. One should learn the theory and put it into practice. Indeed, this is implicit amongst those who wish to make a science out of teaching. Someone, on the basis of research, would be expected to discover the right formulae for effective practice – what makes an effective school or head teacher, how one might effectively control the class, how best to explain fractions, etc.

'Theory' would seem to have the following features. It refers to a set of propositions which are stated with sufficient generality yet precision that they explain the 'behaviour' of a range of phenomena and predict what would happen in future. An understanding of those propositions includes an understanding of what would refute them – or at least what would count as evidence against their being true. The range of propositions would, in that way, be the result of a lot of argument, experiment and criticism. They would be what have survived the constant attempt to refute them. But they would always be provisional. A theory or a set of interconnected and explanatory propositions would be suggestive of hypotheses which need to be tested out. Hence, a theoretical position is always open to further development through reflection, testing against experience and criticism. The more all embracing the theory (the larger its content) then, of course, the more useful it is. But that very usefulness makes it more vulnerable to criticism. And it may be the case that the variability of context of educational practices makes them less open to such large-scale explanatory accounts.

Claims to 'theory', especially in education, are often rather spurious because they are expressed so vaguely or blandly that it is not at all clear what would count as evidence against them. Indeed, a lot of educational pronouncements are of this kind. Theoretical statements would need a certain level of generality, certainly, but their content would need to be 'significant'; that is, acceptance of the content of such statements would need to make a difference to how one views the world, understands experience or engages in practice.

Furthermore, theories can be more or less adequate. They provide a description of the world which seems to work in most cases. But the exceptions cause problems – the uncurious child that seems to refute the view that all children are naturally curious, the good examination results in schools which had subscribed to the causal link between poverty and low standards. There are various ways in which such exceptions might be dealt with. One could turn a blind eye to them or try to explain them away or accept that one's theoretical position refers only to probabilities – our knowledge being too limited at present to embrace one theoretical position for all possible cases. But one might, as a result of the exceptions, abandon the theory or limit it to a smaller range of cases or adapt it. Hence, there is a gradual growth of understanding and explanatory power through tests against experience, through reconceptualization of the problem and through criticism.

Certain features of 'theory' need to be borne in mind, therefore, as we examine the relation of theory to practice, or as we question whether there is a place for theory in the understanding and improvement of 'educational practice'. First, theory supposes that one can express propositionally one's understanding of that which is to be researched into. Second, those propositions are expressed in such a way that they can be hypothesized and put to the test against experience. Third, the interpretation of those tests and that experience can be examined critically by others in the light of the data. Fourth, although it is desirable to make one's theories as all embracing as possible, it is often necessary to be satisfied with small-scale and rather tentative and provisional theoretical positions. Fifth, therefore, the growth of knowledge lies in the constant formulation of the assumptions and beliefs and in the criticism of these in the light of evidence or their implications.

There is, however, something wrong about the commitment to large-scale theories in education for reasons which have been given in chapter 4. There is, furthermore, something intuitively wrong about theory being formulated prior to practice and as a well-formulated guide to practice. And this has profound implications for educational research. Theory and practice are not necessarily related in this way. Educational practice, as I have argued, embraces an indefinite range of activities. What makes these activities an *educational practice* is the overall intention, through these activities, to promote worthwhile learning. Hence, the practice is partly defined in terms of the intentions, beliefs and values of the teacher and of the institutional and social context within which the teachers perceive their task. Those beliefs and values of the teacher, and the beliefs and values built into the institutional framework within which the teacher is working and from which the teacher receives his or her authority, might or might not be called *theory*, depending on the level of reflection or articulation. A progressive school like A. S. Neill's Summerhill or Dewey's Laboratory School quite clearly had a great deal of theory behind it – a theoretical position about child development, about how young people best learn, about what is really worth learning. But, indeed, much the same could be said of many schools which are run by thoughtful teachers.

Similarly individual teachers could be said to have a great deal of theory implicit within their practice. They come to teaching with a range of beliefs about what motivates young people, what they might profitably learn, how their behaviour in the classroom might be managed, what are the key ideas and concepts in the subject matter which they should teach. Indeed, in this respect, what Keynes said of economists and political philosophers could equally be applied to educational theorists:

The ideas of economists and political philosophers ... are more powerful than is commonly understood. Indeed, the world is ruled by little else. Practical men who believe themselves to be quite exempt from any intellectual influence, are usually the slaves of some defunct economist. (Keynes's *General Theory*, quoted by the Secretary of State, March 2000)

Therefore, to attempt to think about a practice, including an educational practice, as though it is devoid of theory would seem to create an unreal dualism. No practice stands outside a theoretical framework – that is, a framework of interconnected beliefs about the world, human beings and the values worth pursuing, which could be expressed propositionally and subjected to critical analysis. To examine practice requires articulating those beliefs and understandings and exposing them to criticism. Such a critique could be pursued in the light of evidence, or conceptual clarification, or the underlying values.

Let me put this point in a slightly different way. To pick out a particular event as an action logically implies reference to the intentions of the agent, and, through a clarification of those, to the theoretical framework of ideas to which the teacher is committed. The distinction which is essential here is that which gives two senses to the question 'Why did you do it?'. Taken in one sense, this could be asking for a causal explanation of the type 'What made you do it?' or 'What was it that happened to you?'. Taken in another sense, however, the questioner would be asking for the reasons why one did it. The questioner could be asking for the teacher to make his behaviour intelligible in terms of the goals, beliefs and values. To ask for reasons in this sense is not to ask for causes. Rather, it presupposes a framework of rules and norms, of aims and purposes within and according to which behaviour is directed – and made intelligible to the outsider. The questioner is seeking to find out the theory behind the practice.

I am not saying that, in practising, the teacher or any agent, prior to making a decision, explicitly goes through a range of mental calculations such as reflecting on overall aims, translating them into objectives and estimating the most likely means of obtaining those objectives. To act intentionally does not require a conscious entertainment of such factors or indeed of the fact that one is intending to do anything prior to or during the intentional activity. Rather, it requires that, in response to the question 'What are you doing?', one would be able to give an answer in those terms, and that, if one could not, one could not be said to be *doing* anything at all (although one might speak of something happening to one as in the case of a reflex action or of being overcome by emotion).

If this is a correct analysis of what is involved in practice, whether educational or otherwise, then it would be a point of entry into the relating of theory to practice. It would also point to the role of philosophy in the determination of practical activities. For if engagement in some practice has an implicit reference to a theoretical position or a particular way of conceptualizing things, however roughly and unreflectively these are held, then one's actions are limited by the limitations of that theoretical framework. (A teacher, for example, who believes in the innate sense of curiosity of all children, even if he or she has never consciously thought about it, will identify and pursue an 'educational practice' in a different way from those who don't.)

Moreover, in so far as the way in which one classifies or conceptualizes reality is built into the language one uses, so too the limits of one's language are the limits of what one might intend and strive for. The elaboration of language, the refinement and differentiation of the way in which we conceptualize and describe experience, is at the same time the extension of possibilities in what one might intend to do. Reading and discussing other people's way of looking at things makes this enlargement and enrichment possible and likely. Reading 'theory' opens the eyes to other possibilities. Perhaps that is one reason why those who run educational systems are so distrustful of theory.

Educational practices, therefore, and the pursuit of educational policies, cannot be understood except within the system of thought – the theoretical framework – which makes them intelligible as practices and as policies. To act intelligently requires reflection upon this framework of ideas. Such a reflection is in part a logical analysis of the implications of the beliefs and assumptions within one's practice. Philosophy is concerned with the implications of what one says and believes, with the conditions for making statements of a certain sort and with how one might distinguish between true and false, intelligible and unintelligible beliefs. Philosophy, therefore, is central to the understanding of educational practices – rendering them intelligible. Failure to examine the logical framework within which one is practising means that one fails to formulate the assumptions upon which one picks out certain goals rather than others or adopts those values which one is subscribing to.

To illustrate these points, one might think of the range of answers that a teacher might give to the question 'What are you doing?'. Eventually the teacher, having explained what she is doing but still not having satisfied her questioner – not because it was an incorrect account but because each answer simply opened up other questions – might in exasperation say that that was what she *meant* by education. Then the conversation would either terminate or become philosophical.

To focus the analysis, by contrast, upon the meaning of educational theory and to trace from *that* analysis the connection with educational practice, as researchers have traditionally tried to do, does not do justice to this conceptual connection between thought and action which analysis of 'practice' would seem to demand. To act at all commits one implicitly to a conceptual scheme with underlying rules of reference and classification and valuation; to *account for one's action* commits one to the articulation of reasons within such a scheme within which the reasons put forward are made intelligible. In other words one is committed, in being 'practical', to theoretical assumptions of some sort; and one is committed, in accounting for one's practice, to some degree of theoretical activity which, if pushed far enough by the questioner or by the self-critical practitioner, will involve essentially philosophical questions about the very intelligibility of one's account and thus of one's action.

Elliott illustrates this theorizing about practice from the Ford Teaching Project which he directed and which involved over 40 teachers in 12 schools. The issue they were addressing was that of methods of teaching which promoted pupil enquiry and discovery. Pupil enquiry and discovery were an alternative mode of learning from that which normally prevailed in classrooms. What starts off with an aspiration, a rather general idea, needs to be translated into a set of practices. And these practices need to be examined. Do they, in fact, embody or make sense of the original aspiration? How far do they depend on classroom organization or previous experience? Do these practices have unintended and unacknowledged effects on the rest of the curriculum?

By sharing the problems, the questions and the tentative conclusions, the teachers were able to build up a body of *professional* knowledge, tentative perhaps, but knowledge which had withstood critical questioning. This professional knowledge was developed through the collection of relevant data (observation by outsiders, tape recording, video), the interpretation of this by observers and participants (including the students) and the critiquing of the interpretation in the light of the evidence (what is referred to as 'triangulation'). Thus, there is a constant interpretation, testing, re-interpretation, critical scrutiny – an ongoing process which feeds into and is put to the test in the teaching.

The consequence of this is thus described by Elliott (1991, p. 32)

> Teachers increasingly observed each other's classrooms, and more requested to be involved in the triangulation. About a third of the teachers embarked on case studies of some aspect of their teaching with a particular class. At the final conference a group of teachers undertook the task of distilling a list of general hypotheses about the problems of implementing inquiry/discover methods from the collective experience ... They were able to describe new insights which had emerged from reflection and discussion about classroom experiences...

In addition, further critical discussion produced hypotheses about educational change, which were themselves tested out in practice – especially hypotheses concerning the potential loss of self-esteem as their practices were subject to critical scrutiny.

I shall return below to these points (see 'Research?') – especially to the questions raised earlier concerning, first, objectivity and impartiality, and, second, the issues concerning generalization. Does 'professional knowledge', unlike scientific knowledge, have to be reinvented or rediscovered all the time? Is there no 'climbing on the shoulders of those who have gone before'? In many ways, it would seem not. What influence have those well-researched projects of the 1960s and 1970s upon curriculum or professional thinking or policy-making now? Perhaps the professional knowledge, based on teachers' own research, remains important only for that group of teachers themselves. It is the kind of knowledge which needs constantly to be reinvented or rediscovered. There may be no other way.

ACTION RESEARCH

Respect for the 'educational practitioners' has given rise to the development of 'action research'. According to Schön, 1995 (quoted by Anderson and Herr, 1999): 'the new scholarship [implies] a kind of action research with norms of its own, which will conflict with the norms of technical rationality – the prevailing epistemology built into the research universities' (p. 27). Thus, the Ford Teaching Project was designed as teacher-based action research. As Elliott stated: 'Teaching was viewed as a form of educational research and the latter as a form of teaching. In other words the two activities were integrated conceptually into a reflective and reflexive practice' (p. 30).

Action research, according to Elliott, is to be contrasted with research, as it is normally understood, in this way. The goal of research is normally that of producing new knowledge. There will, of course, be many different motives for producing such knowledge. But what makes it research is the systematic search for conclusions about 'what is the case' on the basis of relevant evidence. Such conclusions might, indeed, be tentative, always open to further development and refinement. But the purpose remains that of getting ever 'nearer the truth'. Hence, it makes sense to see the outcomes of research to be a series of propositions which are held to be true.

By contrast, the research called 'action research' aims not to produce new knowledge but to improve practice – namely, in this case, the 'educational practice' which teachers are engaged in. The conclusion is not a set of propositions but a practice or a set of transactions or activities which is not true or false but better or worse. By contrast with the conclusion of research, as that is normally conceived, action research focuses on the particular. Although such a practical conclusion focuses on the particular, thereby not justifying generalization, no one situation is unique in every respect and therefore the action research in one classroom or school can *illuminate* or be suggestive of practice elsewhere. There can be, amongst networks of teachers, the development of a body of professional knowledge of 'what works' or of how values might be translated into practice – or come to be transformed by practice. But there is a sense in which such professional knowledge has constantly to be tested out, reflected upon, adapted to new situations.

Research, as that is normally understood, requires a 'research forum' – a group of people with whom the conclusions can be tested out and examined critically. Without such openness to criticism, one might have missed the evidence or the counter argument which casts doubt on the conclusions drawn. Hence, the importance of dissemination through publications and seminars. To think otherwise is to assume a certitude which cannot be justified. Progress in knowledge arises through replication of the research activity, through criticism, through the active attempt to find evidence *against* one's conclusions.

Similarly, the growth of professional knowledge requires the sympathetic but critical community through which one can test out ideas, question the values which underpin the shared practice, seek solutions to problems, invite observation of one's practice, suggest alternative perspectives and interpretation of the data.

This is an important matter to emphasize. The temptation very often is to seek to justify and to verify, rather than to criticize or to falsify, one's belief, and to protect oneself by *not* sharing one's conclusions or the way in which one reached them. Therefore, the criticisms of a lot of educational research by Tooley and Darby (1998), namely, that the methods of selecting or gathering evidence are often not sufficiently clear as to permit criticism, were perfectly valid. Research conclusions are drawn in the light of evidence, and, for them to be accepted by others, there needs to be openness to the way in which evidence is obtained.

Similarly with action research: the active reflection upon practice with a view to its improvement needs to be a public activity. By 'public' I mean that the research is conducted in such a way that others can scrutinize and, if necessary, question the practice of which it is part. Others become part of the reflective process – the identification and definition of the problem, the values which are implicit within the practice, the way of implementing and gathering evidence about the practice, the interpretation of the evidence. And yet teacher research, in the form of action research, is so often encouraged and carried out as a lonely, isolated activity. Those who are concerned with the promotion of action research – with the development in teachers of well-tested professional knowledge – must equally be concerned to develop the professional networks and communities in which it can be fostered.

There is a danger that such research might be supported and funded with a view to knowing the most effective ways of attaining particular goals – goals or targets set by government or others external to the transaction which takes place between teacher and learner. The teacher researches the most efficient means of reaching a particular educational objective (laid out, for instance, in the National Curriculum or a skills-focused vocational training). But this is not what one would have in mind in talking about research as part of professional judgement or action research as a response to a practical issue or problem. The reflective teacher comes to the problem with a set of values. The problem situation is one which raises issues as much about those values as it does about adopting an appropriate means to a given end. Thus, what makes this an *educational* practice is the set of values which it embodies – the intrinsic worth of the activities themselves, the personal qualities which are enhanced, the appropriate way of proceeding (given the values that one has and given the nature of the activity).

One comes to science teaching, for example, with views about the appropriate way of *doing* science – evidence-based enquiry, openness to contrary evidence, clarity of procedures and conclusions. The *practice* of teaching embodies certain values – the importance of that which is to be learnt, the respect for the learner (how he or she thinks), the respect for evidence and the acknowledgement of contrary viewpoints. Therefore, when teacher researchers are putting into practice a particular strategy or are implementing a curriculum proposal, then they are testing out the values as much as the efficaciousness of the strategy or proposal. Are the values the researchers believe in being implemented in the practice? If not, does this lead to shifts in the values espoused or in the practice itself? Action research, in examining the implementation of a curriculum proposal, involves, therefore, a critique of the values which are intrinsic to the practice. Such a critique will reflect the values which the teacher brings to the practice, and those values will in turn be refined through critical reflection upon their implementation in practice. 'Action research' captures this ever-shifting conception of practice through the attempt to put into practice certain procedures which one believes are educational.

However, such constant putting into practice, reflecting on that practice, refining of beliefs and values in the light of that reflection, subjecting the embodied ideas to criticism, cannot confine itself to the act of teaching itself. It cannot but embrace the context of teaching – the physical conditions in which learning is expected to take place, the expectations of those who determine the general shape of the curriculum, the resources available for the teachers to draw upon, the constraints upon the teacher's creative response to the issues, the scheme of assessment. It is difficult to see how the clash between the 'official curriculum' and the 'teacher researcher' can be avoided when the latter is constantly testing out the values of the teaching strategies. One can see, therefore, why the encouragement of teacher research is so often defined within official documents in a rather narrow sense.

Action research, therefore, is proposed as a form of research in which teachers review their practice in the light of evidence and of critical judgement of others. In so doing, they inevitably examine what happens to the values they hold, and which they regard as intrinsic to the transaction they are engaged in. Such critical appraisal of practice takes in three different factors which impinge upon practice, and shape the activities within it – the perceptions and values of the different participants, the 'official expectations and values' embodied within the curriculum, and the physical conditions and resources. To do this, various methods for gathering data will be selected – examination results, classroom observation, talking with the pupils. And the interpretation of what is 'working' will constantly be revised in the light of such data. But, of course, others too might, in the light of the data, suggest other possible interpretations. Thus, the dialogue continues. There is no end to this systematic reflection with a view to improving practice.

RESEARCH?

We need, however, to reflect on what would seem to be the necessary conditions for such teacher reflection to be considered as research. Is the word 'research' being used too elastically when extended to 'teacher research' or 'action research' – to the 'improvement of practice' rather than to the 'production of knowledge'? Does the concentration upon the uniqueness and distinctiveness of an 'educational practice' preclude the relevance of research as that is normally understood (and as that is required by 'evidence-based policy and practice')?

First, research implies some sort of truth-claim, however tentative and limited in its application – even if such a claim is about the improvement of practice. The distinction between research aimed at the production of knowledge and research aimed at the improvement of practice is much more blurred than Elliott assumed. Therefore, all research, including teacher research, leads to conclusions expressed in such a way that they can be tested in experience, critically scrutinized, examined for consistency with other beliefs and practices. Such conclusions should be related to evidence in a way that is also open to scrutiny and criticism. Of course, for the very reasons raised in this book, the conclusions of teacher research would usually be limited in their application. Context, teacher perceptions and beliefs, learner aspirations and interpretations of the situation, all affect the way in which curriculum intentions are realized in practice. But there are sufficient similarities between contexts, and there is often sufficient agreement on understandings and values, for well-tested hypotheses in one situation to illuminate similar practice undertaken by others. Furthermore, part of such research would be to delineate those distinctive features of the situation which limit the possibility of generalization. Hence, as in any research, that conducted by the teacher with a view to the improvement of practice should lead to a growth of knowledge, even if this is context bound, tentative, provisional and constantly open to improvement. The teacher researcher is engaged in an enquiry which can be shared fruitfully with other teachers but which can reach no final conclusion.

Second, 'objectivity' must be an essential feature of this, as indeed of any research. Objectivity lies in the systematic and open attempt to check the interpretation of what happens against the evidence. It lies, too, in the checking with other people as to whether those interpretations are the most appropriate ones in the light of the data. One might ask, for example, whether such data could support other interpretations. One might question the ways in which the data was obtained, the representative nature of the sample, the relevance of that kind of evidence to that kind of conclusion. 'Objectivity' is achieved in taking the necessary steps to eliminate bias or subjective interpretations of the evidence, and that is ensured by seeking wide and continuous criticism of the conclusions provisionally reached. Research, therefore, requires a research culture, an atmosphere in which criticism is welcome rather than avoided and a forum in which others are in a position to examine conclusions in the light of evidence. Such a culture, too, would ensure that the skills and resources for collecting the data were made available – for instance, the group of sympathetic but critical teachers who provide different and challenging perspectives. However, such conditions for objectivity rarely obtain, even where teacher research is claimed to be encouraged. In many respects, such openness to criticism goes against the grain. We tend to defend our point of view rather than seek criticism; to treat the beliefs that we hold with confidence, if not certainty, rather than with the systematic doubt which motivates the researcher.

Third, within such a research framework, there will, through the interactions between those exploring the questions, develop a common set of understandings, a common theoretical framework, if you like, so that one piece of classroom research might shed light on other, similarly conceived situations. Such a common theoretical framework is reached through argument, criticism, questioning. Research is as much about conceptualizing the problem as it is about collecting data. The researchers are testing assumptions about the implications for practice of their educational intentions or their interpretations of what has been prescribed for them. Those assumptions will include not only the most effective means for reaching some prescribed goal but also the educational values which they want to transmit. Hence, as researchers they will be engaged in an ethical debate as well as an empirical enquiry. And in doing so, they will develop case studies which illuminate similar endeavours and similar ethical issues.

* * *

The criticisms of educational research referred to at the beginning of this book have led to scepticism about the value and validity of educational research which does not involve the teachers themselves – the 'situated cognition' which Putnam and Borko refer to. And, therefore, there is renewed interest in teacher and action research. In Britain, the Teacher Training Agency, following the arguments of Hargreaves (1996) in which he talks of the funds for educational research being 'prised out of the academic community' (p. 7), has given money, previously granted to universities, to the teachers themselves to undertake research. The idea is to develop a 'research-based profession'.

There are, however, three issues which need to be raised about such a development in the light of the points made in this chapter.

First, the research encouraged by the Agency concerns 'what effective teachers do and/or how they become effective'. Further-more, such research should 'add to the existing stock of knowledge available to teachers and the research community' (Teacher Training Agency, 1996). On both counts, however, such a conception of teacher research is questionable. The teacher researcher, in examining his or her practice from a professional point of view, will be questioning the agenda set as much as the most effective way of meeting that agenda. There will be, inevitably, in the public scrutiny of the 'educational practice', an exploration of the values of the practice as much as the effectiveness of the activities within it. Judgements are about goals as well as the means which embody those goals.

Second, despite the criticisms which Hargreaves and others level against academic research, they feel certain that the accumulation of knowledge, as in medicine, is both possible and desirable. But the growth of 'professional knowledge' within shared frameworks of ideas and values has, by contrast, to be tentative and context bound. Such bits of knowledge, even when added to lots of other bits, cannot become the context-free knowledge which permit the law-like generalizations wanted by government and systematic reviewers.

Third, such research would need to meet the criteria outlined above, namely, first, tentative conclusions stated with sufficient clarity that they can be tested against experience; second, an explicit relation of such conclusions to relevant evidence; third, a process of public scrutiny of procedures, of questioning of the values; fourth, a testing of alternative interpretations of the data which may support more than one conclusion. Research requires a community of researchers, an openness to public criticism, a sharing of ideas and of explanations. Otherwise how will one know if one has got it wrong?

An important critique of the 'teacher as researcher' development has been given by Foster (1999). He scrutinized 25 summaries and 16 reports of the teacher research funded by the Teacher Training Agency in 1996/97 with help of grants averaging £2000. Foster defined research as

> the production of knowledge ... pursued by the employment of systematic and rigorous methods of data collection and analysis. This definition includes what is sometimes termed 'action research' as well as more traditional forms of enquiry. The key difference is that in the former the knowledge produced usually has more immediate relevance to the practitioners involved because it is focused directly on their practice and changes in this.

This definition is in agreement with the conditions which, I argued, seem essential to any enquiry which is called research. By implication, access to public scrutiny and critique is included. And Foster argues, as I have also argued, that the distinction between 'production of knowledge' and 'improvement of practice', as a basis for distinguishing between 'normal' and 'action' research, is unacceptable. 'Action research' is concerned with the production of knowledge, albeit tentatively and with a view to changing the situation in which, for a time, the knowledge claims were true. In other words, it is not enough in defending teacher *research*, to claim that practice had improved. It is necessary for there to be knowledge of why it improved.

In the light of this, Foster concluded that much of the purported teacher research could not justifiably be called research. Claims that the 'research activities' or interventions led to improvement in practice may be true, but that is not enough. The problems lay, however, mainly in the accessibility to the evidence on which the conclusions were based – to the lack of public scrutiny of the link between data and conclusions or to a lack of clarity in the testability in practice of the conclusions drawn from the data. There is a contrast to be made between the claims being made by those responsible for this development and those of the Ford Teaching Project where a much more systematic, public and critical framework was developed by groups of teachers with a view to building up their professional knowledge.

CONCLUSION

The notion of the teacher as researcher is important. It is crucial to the growth of professional knowledge. It is a refinement of the intelligent engagement in an 'educational practice'. It is a refreshing counterbalance to those who, in treating 'educational practice' as an object of science, necessarily fail to understand it. It is reassertion of the crucial place of professional judgement in an understanding of a professional activity.

However, two *caveats* arise from this analysis. The first is that the distinctive features of the growth of professional knowledge do not excuse research, which leads to it, from the conditions of good research which I have outlined. Research is more than intelligent action or reflective practice. It is more, even, than an extension of these. It requires a context of openness, public scrutiny and criticism. And, as Foster demonstrates, what is often claimed to be teacher research does not match up to these criteria.

The second *caveat* is this. There is here, as elsewhere, the danger once again of falling into the trap of drawing too sharp a contrast between different kinds of research of creating false dualisms. It is as though either that educational research can be modelled on that of the social *sciences* (and thus ignore the subtle differences between contexts) or that such research should be focused on the uniqueness of each educational practice (thereby eschewing the generalizations which arise from large-scale surveys). But there is a middle way. No situation is unique in every respect. Educational practices are conducted or engaged in within societies of shared values and understandings. There are national, indeed global debates, which create common understandings. And there are generalizations about how people are motivated and learn, however tentative these must be and in need of testing in the circumstances of particular classrooms. Reviews of such general conclusions of large-scale research should not dictate how this or that policy is to prevail, or how this or that professional practice should be adopted. But the deliberations of policy-makers and practitioners should take such conclusions into account as they deliberate the best way forward. Research is the servant of professional judgement, not its master.

—7—

Ethical dimensions to educational research

ETHICS

Reference to 'ethical implications' is frequently required by those who sponsor research. And most theses reserve a section for these. But the word 'ethics' is used loosely. It is often used interchangeably with morals.

Normally a distinction is drawn by philosophers between 'morals' (concerned with what is the right or wrong thing to do) and ethics (the philosophical enquiry into the basis of morals or moral judgement). Translated into the language of educational research, 'ethics' for Simons (1995, p. 436) refers to the 'search for rules of conduct that enable us to operate defensibly in the political contexts in which we have to conduct educational research'. Perhaps this is unnecessarily narrow in its focus on the political context. But the 'search for rules' is at least one important ethical dimension to any consideration of human behaviour.

This chapter is more concerned with the meaning and justification of moral considerations which underlie research, than it is with making any particular moral judgements. Indeed, one conclusion will be that moral judgements or decisions require a great deal of deliberation in the light of many factors which have to be taken into account. There is rarely a clear-cut, and context-free, set of rules or principles which can be applied without deliberation and judgement. Moral thinking is a kind of practical thinking, and thus the educational researcher faces the same kind of moral demands as does the teacher as he or she applies professional judgement in the 'educational practice'. There is a constant need to reflect on the values which inform the research and the ways in which those values might be made concrete in the research activity itself.

There are different kinds of moral considerations which enter into deliberations about the conduct of research. I want to make a distinction between those considerations which relate to general 'principles of action' and those which relate to the dispositions and character of the researcher.

With regard to the former, there is a long tradition in ethics which focuses upon the nature of moral judgement and upon what counts as a relevant reason for coming to one kind of conclusion rather than another. Thus moral questions, on this view, arise from the question 'What ought I to do?'. Such a question might be purely practical or 'prudential' of the kind 'What is the most effective way of demonstrating the solution to this problem in mathematics?'. But it may be as much about the ends to be pursued as about the means of achieving those ends. In this case one is asking about the values which one should be trying to make concrete in one's action.

This search for the appropriate reasons for acting in one way rather than another, where that search is concerned with the values worth pursuing, might be expressed in statements of principle. Principles are what one appeals to in justifying an action. Furthermore, they have built into them a universality of application. The *principle* of acting in this way rather than another does not depend upon my whims or wishes; anyone in like circumstances would be expected to act in a similar way. Thus, in pursuing the question 'Why should you adopt this policy rather than that, or behave towards someone in that manner rather than another?', eventually one would appeal to some general principle such as 'One ought to act in this way because it is likely to make people happy' or 'One should always tell the truth' or 'One should so act towards others as one would wish that they would act towards oneself' or 'On matters of public policy, the public has a right to know'. (Of course, one can always refuse to pursue these questions – to opt out of any form of principled life whatsoever. But that would be difficult to sustain for very long, never able to appeal to principles of justice or fairness, for example, when one feels wronged.)

A distinction is to be made between 'principles' and 'rules'. 'Rules' are more specific and less open to interpretation. Thus, the sponsors may insist upon specific rules about the conduct of the sponsored research – when and how it is to be presented, or how exactly it is to be conducted. Such rules are of the kind 'In circumstances X, one must do Y'. There is little ambiguity or openness to interpretation. The rest of life is constrained by such rules (for example, in the everyday activity of driving, 'Keep to the left hand side of the road' or 'Never overtake on a double white line') and in that respect one should expect nothing different where research is being conducted. But behind such rules may be general principles, such as 'One ought to drive in such a way as not to cause harm to others'. Similarly, behind the rules for the conduct of research may be principles of the kind 'The research ought to answer the questions asked by the sponsors' or 'The research ought to take account of the possible harm it might do to those who are the objects of the research', which is then translated into the rules for the actual conduct of the research.

Principles, then, have the logic of general rules, but they embody the values appealed to in the establishment of the rules or in the questioning of the appropriateness of the rules on this or that occasion. This is important because there is a temptation, in recognizing the moral and political dilemmas over the conduct and the dissemination of research, to establish rules of conduct. But that would be a mistake. Here, as in any moral conflict, there is no way in which rules can be established for every conceivable situation. What is essential is the clarification of principles which then need to be applied to particular situations, in the full knowledge that other principles might also be evoked which would lead to different decisions. There is no avoiding moral deliberation.

The list of 'basic' principles could be very large. But one can make a major distinction between principles which highlight the consequences of an action and those which, irrespective of the consequences, insist upon certain basic rules of conduct. The pursuit of happiness as the ultimate goal looks to the consequences of one's actions as a justification; telling the truth or behaving justly emphasises basic rules of conduct – values which should guide how one behaves in different circumstances.

There lies a difficulty, on any one occasion, in deciding what should be the overriding principle, because the principles often clash with each other. To tell the truth may lead to a great deal of unhappiness. Respect for a person's dignity might lead, in some cases, to telling uncomfortable truths but, in other cases, concealing them. The history of ethics is the history of philosophers giving preference to certain general principles over others. Thus the utilitarians attach supreme importance to the creation of the greatest amount of happiness for the greatest number. Others subscribe to the supremacy of justice and fairness. Others, again, put 'respect for persons' at the centre of moral deliberation. The ethical dimension of research involves, as we shall see, this complexity of ethical debate. And the researcher is caught up in a process of deliberation which too often is not recognized for the complex moral and practical debate that it is. Either they fail to see the moral dimension of what they are doing, or they apply rather dogmatically one principle (for example, telling the truth irrespective of consequences) to the exclusion of others.

The principles which seem particularly important to educational research but often irreconcilable, are, first, the principle which requires respect for the dignity and confidentiality of those who are the 'objects' of research, and, second, the principle which reflects the purpose of research, namely, the pursuit of truth. The significance of this I shall deal with in the next section, but of course it will raise interesting questions about the rights of those sponsors who have funded the research.

So much at the moment, therefore, for the importance of 'principled thinking' about research – namely, what are to count as good reasons for making this or that decision. But there is another approach to ethical questions which is rarely mentioned in the conduct of or in the literature on educational research, namely, the appropriate dispositions or attitudes of the researcher. Good actions are what good people do. On the whole we act from character or from our dispositions to see, value and behave in a certain way. Excellence in canon law does not guarantee virtuous action; nor does the incapacity to carry through the complex reasoning of the canon lawyer debar one from living a fully moral life. Indeed, moral education, it might be argued, should concentrate more upon the nurturing of the virtues than upon the development of moral reasoning. By 'virtue' I mean the *disposition* to act appropriately in a particular situation. There are moral virtues and intellectual virtues (and some would also want to add theological virtues). Moral virtues are dispositions like courage, kindness, generosity of spirit, honesty, concern for justice – indeed, very much the Sermon on the Mount with a few additions due to changes in circumstance. Intellectual virtues would refer to concern to find out the truth and not to cook the books, openness to criticism, an interest in clarity of communication, a concern for evidence. When one acts or makes practical judgements, generally one acts or judges from the deep-seated dispositions which are part of one's very being. And so the deliberation, which is inevitable in the complexity of practical situations and the clash of principles which I have spoken of, will be greatly determined by the dispositions or virtues of the researcher.

Ought one, then, in selecting educational researchers, to look more to the relevant virtues than to the skills and knowledge required for doing research? Of course, one could ask the same question about the selection of teachers. However clever they are and knowledgeable about the subject they are to teach, they need the right dispositions towards the students if they are, in the many interactions with them, to make the appropriate professional judgement. The third section of this chapter will examine, therefore, the virtues of the good educational researcher.

Finally, however, research takes place within a framework of community values. By 'community' I mean the larger social framework within which the transactions between teacher and learner take place. Too often the analysis of and prescriptions for moral education focus entirely on the individual – the qualities, skills, knowledge and dispositions which persons need to develop if they are to live a fully moral life. But we know from the work of Kohlberg and others that this is not the way forward. Virtue generally develops in a society (the family, the school, the neighbourhood, etc.) which values those virtues and incorporates them into its own form of life. (See Kohlberg, 1982, and Power and Reimer, 1978.) Researchers, too, can easily be led to see things as the wider society sees them, particularly where a government, with a specific agenda and thinking in business terms, sets the conditions for research funding. This I shall examine in the final section.

PRINCIPLES

The overriding principle which informs research would seem to be that of 'finding the truth'. This is much more than 'telling the truth', although it does of course include that. The purpose of undertaking research is the production of new knowledge. The reasons for seeking new knowledge are several: the improvement of practice, a knowledge-base for developing policy, increased accountability, solving problems which the researchers find interesting. The reasons, however, are not the most important point for the moment. The characterization of research as the production of new knowledge is.

The production of new knowledge requires access to the relevant data. Researchers, therefore, provide a *prima facie* case for having the right to such access, and for wider circulation both of the data and of the conclusions drawn from them. Without such access and without the right to a more public forum, one will never know what is the case. Growth of knowledge comes through criticism.

The 'right to know' seems all the more urgent where matters of public interest are concerned. Such matters of public interest include the effectiveness of the educational institutions, the success or otherwise of policy initiatives and interventions, the adoption of particular teaching methods. One can see, therefore, the resistance to research from those in positions of power. Research seeks to get at the truth where the truth might hurt. Research exposes the secrecy which so often permeates the conduct of affairs by public institutions such as schools, local authorities, government depart-ments and committees. But there is a need for more openness to ensure that decisions are informed by the most up-to-date knowl-edge and understanding and that the institutions are properly accountable to the people that they serve. There would seem to be, therefore, a *prima facie* case for claiming the 'right to know' and for the exercise of this right through a more thorough research and evaluation of the system and practices of education. Moreover, it would seem to be essential that such research should remain independent of those who might benefit from or be disadvantaged by it, lest the conclusions drawn reflect the interests of the sponsors rather than the pursuit of the truth wherever that leads. Such is the importance of this principle that it might be considered to be overriding, even when the research and its revelations damage the people and the institutions enquired into.

Goldstein and Myers (1996, p. 13) quote the quite uncompromis-ing statement to this effect by the Inner London Education Authority in 1987:

> The requirement to publish examination results inevitably involves the risk of institutional damage. However, if such data are not made available it is possible that schools will not be aware of their current performance in relation to other schools, and therefore there will be less pressure for improvement of current practices ... We conclude that the determining factor should be the right of parents to have the most useful information.

Such a statement could apply to the defence of much research where the consequences might be seen to hurt the individuals concerned. In an age of increased accountability, there will inevitably be some casualties.

The pursuit of knowledge, and the associated right to know, is not a principle (like that concerned with the pursuit of happiness) which looks to the consequences of an action. Rather is it a principle of procedure which seems intrinsic to the very engagement in research. The justification for such a principle is implicit in John Stuart Mill's argument in his essay *On Liberty* (1859) for preserving and extending freedom of discussion:

> the peculiar evil of silencing the expression of an opinion is, that it is robbing the human race; posterity as well as the present generation; those who dissent from the opinion, still more than those who hold it. If the opinion is right, they are deprived of the opportunity of exchanging error for truth; if wrong, they lose, what is almost as great a benefit, the clearer perception and livelier impression of truth, produced by its collision with error. (p. 142)

Accessibility of information is a precondition of a proper discussion of any opinion, policy or practice. Therefore, there is, on Mill's argument, a *prima facie* case for establishing the right to know as a basic one in any society, if either the eradication of error or the greater clarity of the truth is valued – as indeed it must be by anyone who seriously engages in enquiry or research. There are no absolute certainties, and thus, faced with the continual possibility of self-deception or of mistaken conclusions, one should welcome rather than spurn the well-researched criticism or proposal.

However, I find myself constantly referring to the *prima facie* right to know. Moral situations are nearly always complicated because rival considerations bear upon the situation. Three come to mind.

First, one can never forget completely the consequences of what one is doing, however righteous one might feel about the principles according to which one is proceeding. There are consequences for the school or the teachers in an exposition of what the research concludes. Does the researcher have to balance the right to know against the possible harm which might follow from the research – the demoralization of the teacher or the drop in recruitment to the school which might follow from the conduct and dissemination of the research? There are duties of respect to those who are being researched, often people in positions of vulnerability.

Second, there is the possibility of a clash between the right to know and the commitment to confidentiality over the source, and sometimes content, of what has been gathered from the enquiry.

And there are no higher level principles to be appealed to for resolving that clash. Such accounts are often obtainable only under conditions of confidentiality. Even where such confidentiality is not formally agreed, the researcher may feel obliged, given the vulnerability of those who are interviewed, to treat what is heard with sensitivity and care. Interviewees might justifiably feel aggrieved if matters are revealed where they had not realized the full impact of the revelation. A trust established might be considered betrayed – just as the repetition to others of intimate conversations between friends would be considered a betrayal. Formal agreements of confidentiality are not essential to relationships of trust. And this is even more the case given the relatively vulnerable position of the interviewee in relationship to the researcher. It is the former, not the latter, who makes the revelations; but the other way around in decisions about what goes public.

Third, given the provisional nature of all truth claims, it is always possible that, in the light of further argument and evidence, the conclusions of the research may need to be reviewed. Therefore, the researcher ought to be tentative and modest in what he or she claims to have found out. Rarely does research provide the definitive word on anything. Much better if it were treated as the provisional conclusion, the most thoroughly corroborated position in the light of available evidence, open to yet further correction and refinement, a part of the 'conversation' which is essential to intelligent policy-making and professional judgement. Or, indeed, the research and its interpretation may be so complex that the inevitable public interpretation of it will be misleading. As Goldstein and Myers (1996) argue:

> much of what might be described as performance indicators – statements about schools or other institutions – falls into this category. Its ability to reflect objective reality may be extremely limited and its publication may therefore cause incorrect inferences about institutions to be drawn ... In such circumstances, we would argue, there is a strong case for withholding publication. (p. 13/14)

But even where publication cannot be stopped, it ought to carry 'health warnings' – an explanation of the limits and tentativeness of the research findings, and the possibility of error. A major argument of this book has been that, due to the complexity of social reality and the privileged position of the participants in understanding them, the outsider might not grasp the truth in all its complexity. Indeed, it is for this reason that the accounts given by the 'insiders' are so important.

These difficulties in conceding an absolute 'right to know' are already suggestive of ways forward in establishing principles for the conduct of research, albeit principles which, like all moral principles, need to be translated into rules of action through careful deliberation in the light of the particular context.

There is a *prima facie* case for 'the right to know' – for access to whatever evidence or data will enable the researcher to get at the truth. But immediately there are 'caveats'. The researcher must have good reason for undertaking the research. The task takes up the teachers' and the school's time, say. And any sensible head teacher would weigh up the overall good which accrues from the research. 'Negotiating access' is an important task of the researcher, and part of that task will be agreement about conditions on which the research is to be conducted. Getting that agreement raises the very ethical questions I pointed to concerning confidentiality, respect for the teacher, possible harm to the school, misuse of half-understood truth claims. Above all, the head would need to be assured that the researcher had the relevant virtues. Right action, in complex moral deliberations, stems from the right dispositions.

To that extent, research requires negotiation over procedures. Such negotiation would refer to: first, the extent to which the anonymity of the school and teachers needs to be and can be preserved – not an easy matter; second, the ways in which the information is to be gathered; third, clearance with relevant people of this information as accurate and acceptable reflections of what was said or seen; fourth, an opportunity for all concerned to question the researcher's interpretation of the data; finally, the right of those concerned to offer an alternative interpretation of the evidence.

The importance attached to 'negotiation' has been argued by MacDonald (1974), and no doubt many others, to arise from a 'democratic' style of research and evaluation. The arguments for 'democracy' seem to be two.

First, there is the principle of 'respect for persons' – the recognition that those being researched also have certain rights, in particular, the right not to be unnecessarily harmed in the exercise of their duties.

Second, there is the principle that one should respect those conditions which are necessary for getting at the truth. Such conditions include the right to check the accuracy of reports on matters to which the teachers, say, have privileged access and the right to offer alternative interpretations of the evidence or data. We return again and again, in considering the ethical dimension of research, to the nature of knowledge, its provisional status in the light of current evidence, the likelihood of further development in the light of new discoveries, and the necessary link between openness to criticism and the growth of knowledge.

None the less, a word of caution is required. There is something odd about the term 'negotiation', much loved by educational researchers, especially those within the 'postmodern embrace'. It is a metaphor taken from business, and like all metaphors it plays its part but has its limitations. Particularly, however, it is odd in an area where matters of truth and falsity are concerned, and there is often a confusion between negotiating the release of knowledge (or negotiating the conditions under which knowledge might be pursued) and negotiating what is to count as knowledge. Quite clearly, from my argument in chapter 4, the latter simply does not make sense. But the former, namely, the negotiation of the conditions for the pursuit of knowledge, has its difficulties also. There are good and bad negotiators and the process of negotiation here, as in business, depends so often on the power of the negotiators. Hence, the ethics and the politics of research become intertwined. How far can one ensure confidentiality or clearance of research findings without jeopardizing the objectivity and independence of the research? Have not those who want to know the truth (parents, say) as much right as teachers to prevent harm being done? What certainly is clear is that the further one extends the right to confidentiality and the consequent obligation to 'negotiate', the greater must be the constraints upon the 'right to know'.

What then would be the kind of general principles which would reconcile these various moral demands, albeit only through the deliberations about applicability to particular cases?

First, the researcher should set out clearly the *kinds* of knowledge required. It is of course impossible in research to anticipate all the kinds of information which may be of interest, but those being researched would seem to have a right to know beforehand what in general terms the researchers would be looking for and for what purpose. There would also be the continuing opportunity to renegotiate the terms of the research contract as the research revealed new avenues for enquiry or new sources of information which could not have been anticipated at the beginning.

Second, depending of course on the specific purposes of the research, the institutions and people should be made anonymous, though this may be difficult in some instance because of the necessity to contextualize the research. Furthermore, it may be necessary within some institutions to check, with the people being researched, the data and the conclusions before they are conveyed to others. This is an extension of the principle of trust and confidentiality, as well as an assurance that the research has taken steps to ensure accuracy and defensibility of its interim findings.

Third, the researcher would be open to cross-examination by those at the receiving end of the research – the main purposes and objectives, the research methods, the political implications of the research, the data collected and the interpretations being put upon that data. Such obligations arise from the ill-conceived nature of some research, and from the fact that all knowledge is so from a particular point of view. It is selective. There may be other perspectives and other interpretations of the data which should be considered.

Fourth, the research should provide a space for the right to reply from those who have participated in the research but who may believe that alternative conclusions could be supported by the data. No one is infallible, let alone researchers, and confidence in research is increased if there is openness to criticism and alternative interpretations.

Fifth, in terms of 'consequential principles' the researcher cannot ignore the possible ways in which research findings may be used. Research often appears in highly charged political contexts in which the findings are picked out selectively to support different sides of the political spectrum. This creates moral problems for the researcher since it can never be clear beforehand exactly how research will be used. And to play for safety would be to betray others' right to know. Again, this is a matter of weighing in the balance the consequences of publishing against the right of others to know. Certainly, there is an obligation on the researcher to guide the public in its interpretation of the findings.

VIRTUES

Virtues are general dispositions to do the right thing at the right time. Any list of virtues, therefore, embodies the values which prevail in a social or cultural tradition. Chivalry reflected the kind of behaviour expected of a knightly class, and the chivalrous person would, even against difficulty, be disposed so to act in the appropriate circumstances. Obedience is required of subjects in an autocratic society and the virtue consists in being so disposed to act, even when the temptation is to follow one's own wishes. Distributive justice refers to the distribution of scarce goods on the basis of merit and need, and the just or virtuous person would have a strong inclination so to do.

So one might go on with a list of virtues which would constitute our views of the thoroughly virtuous person. Few moral situations require a great deal of deliberation. People act out of their 'natural' inclinations. They see a situation as unjust, and, if they are so disposed, seek to remedy the injustice. A kind person will recognize the hurt done to another and will try to bring comfort. The courageous person will not be disposed to abandon his or her obligations at the sign of danger. It is quite possible for a person to accept the reasons for behaving in a particular way but not be disposed so to act – not to have the relevant virtue. Indeed, such capacity to reason may be put at the disposal of the very feelings which are not virtuous.

The engagement in research is no exception. Clever people, knowing the conclusions they want, can, if so disposed, find the data and arguments to justify them. Research, therefore, requires very special sorts of virtue, both moral and intellectual.

The intellectual virtues concern the disposition to search for the truth even when that might be painful, and impartiality in the face of rival but not equally attractive interpretations and recommendations. The truth is not always kind. And the rewards for its pursuit may be small. Self-interest might suggest cutting corners or being economic with the truth or giving up the search or siding with one viewpoint rather than another. But true researchers would *feel* ill at ease with such behaviours. Such behaviours would go against the deep-down feelings concerning how they ought to act. Such intellectual virtues therefore would include openness to criticism and co-operation since it is the truth which matters more than one's own personal recognition by others. The virtuous researcher would be horrified at any attempt to 'cook the books' or to stifle criticism or to destroy data or to act partially.

The moral virtues would be those concerned with the resistance to the blandishments or attractions which tempt one from the research, even where the intellectual virtues press one to go on: courage to proceed when the research is tough or unpopular;

honesty when the consequences of telling the truth are uncomfortable; concern for the well-being of those who are being researched and who, if treated insensitively, might suffer harm; modesty about the merits of the research and its conclusions; humility in the face of justified criticism and the readiness to take such criticisms seriously.

This can be illustrated in the importance attached to 'trust'. Clear cases of betrayal of trust are where a promise is broken. There is, of course, something peculiar about the *obligation* to keep promises. Where that obligation is not recognized the very meaning of 'making a promise' disintegrates. Little value can be attached to promises where it is understood that the promises can be broken when convenient. Keeping promises would seem to be a *prima facie* duty or principle. However, the trust which is built up between researcher and researched, on the basis of which information is given and intelligence gained, is rarely made explicit in actual promises. It is more a matter of implicit trusting with information, putting oneself in a vulnerable position. This respect for others as vulnerable puts real constraints upon the sensitive evaluator or researcher, however much public importance he or she attaches to the information that has been obtained. It is not possible to say what should be done without examination of the particular case. But the virtuous researcher will be aware of difficulties that others would not be; such a researcher would bring factors into the deliberations which others would omit.

It would be impossible, of course, to contemplate moral tests for potential researchers, but such qualities and dispositions would seem to be essential. And yet they are rarely spoken about. In their absence, it is difficult to see how one can trust the results of research since, so complex is much of it and so dependent on sponsorship, that the temptations are there for the researcher to take short cuts, to do the sponsor's bidding and to serve the public that pays rather than the research community which doesn't.

DEMOCRATIC VALUES

The word 'negotiation', inadequate metaphor though it may be, has reminded us that drawing the boundary between the right to know and the respect for the trust and confidentiality of those being researched cannot be seen outside a political context – outside, that is, a context in which power and influence are exercised over people. There is a *prima facie* case for limiting the importance of confidentiality in research into policy-making (rather than in the research into the professional judgement of the teacher or into the professional environment of the school) where it is so easy for those in power to distort things for their own political purposes. Knowledge is an important ingredient in this exercise of power – and in the exposure of it. But the information industry is as much the servant of *interested* parties as it is the servant of those who, in a disinterested way, are keen to get at the truth.

We are seeing increasingly a greater control over the direction, content and dissemination of research by government, as it pursues its agenda of educational reform. To quote Simons (1995, p. 436):

> The policy context in which we have to conduct educational research sponsored by government in England at the current time has made the politics of research more explicit and contestable than ever before and placed the ethics of research practice under severe constraint, so much so that the quality of educational research is itself under threat, and thereby the contribution it can make to the generation of knowledge and the improvement of educational policy and practice.

'Negotiating' contracts with a researcher or evaluator can be seen as a 'trading' in political power with consequences for a shift in the distribution of knowledge. Knowledge serves a purpose, and the powerful negotiators are the ones who, through one means or another, ensure that the research serves their purposes. Therefore, those researchers who enter into contracts with powerful sponsors, including government departments, need to consider the consequences for the integrity of their research of such contracts. Such considerations would include: the right to report unaltered what arises from the research; the copyright over the research and its data; the right to go public; the choice, after due deliberation, of the appropriate research approach. To what extent is it a matter of what the sponsor pays for, the sponsor owns? The British Educational Research Association (1992), therefore, included amongst its admirable guidelines for the conduct of educational research the following clause:

> Educational researchers should not agree to conduct research that conflicts with academic freedom, nor should they agree to undue or questionable influence by government or other funding agencies. Examples of such improper influence

include endeavours to interfere with the conduct of research, the analysis of findings, or the reporting of interpretations. Researchers should report to BERA attempts by sponsors or funding agencies to use any questionable influence ... (British Educational Research Association, Guideline 16)

Furthermore, with regard to publication:

Researchers have a duty to report to the funding agency and to the wider public, including educational practitioners and other interested parties. The right to publish is therefore entailed by this duty to report. Researchers conducting sponsored research should retain the right to publish the findings under their own names. The right to publish is essential to the long-term viability of any research activity, to the credibility of the researcher ... and in the interests of the open society. (*Ibid.*, Guideline 23)

Similar guidelines were issued about the same time by the American Educational Research Association, published in *Educational Researcher* (1992). Both these and those of BERA reflect the sort of values which ought to pertain in a democratic society amongst which 'openness' would seem to be one. Openness to criticism, open access to relevant information, openness to public debate about issues of public importance – these would seem to be virtues of a democratic society. And, like personal virtues, they need to be carefully nurtured and protected, for it is all too easy for those in power to protect their interests by recourse to secrecy and the stifling of discussion. (See Bridges, 1998, for an excellent account of the moral issues in 'Research for sale'.)

Further than that, however, the values of the society are embodied and conveyed in the language we employ to talk about matters of public concern. I referred in chapter 3 to the shifting language of education – to the 'thinking in business terms' in which educational practice is thought about very differently with its cascaded targets, its efficiency gains and effectiveness measures, its performance indicators and audits, its customers and productivity. And as such it will adopt the 'virtues of the business world', especially those connected with effectiveness, efficiency and enterprise. Such values call for different qualities in the researcher to be employed, and a readiness to serve the bureaucracy rather than to follow up what is essential for a comprehensive and critical account.

The distinctive values and accompanying virtues of the educational researcher remain, albeit in tension with the values and virtues of a non-democratic bureaucracy which increasingly funds and constrains research. And this is a pity because the values of a democratic community would seem to be essential for the tradition of educational research which serves the many interested parties and which can give assurance that, through openness to criticism, it will at least approximate to the truth.

Similarly, such virtues ought to characterize the school community if teachers themselves are to be researchers. As I argued in chapter 6, the teacher researcher needs to be in a community of people with whom problems can be shared, possible solutions identified, ideas and hypotheses put to the test, tentative conclusions reached, and criticism invited both of the conclusions and of the research methods adopted. Such schools need to nurture such research communities, possibly with the assistance of an external moderator.

But that is not easy. Research at any level goes against the grain. The natural tendency is to defend cherished beliefs, not to question too deeply, not to suffer the discomforts of doubt. To reverse such a tendency requires the careful nurturing of different dispositions – the disposition to pursue the truth even when that pursuit reaches conclusions one does not want, the disposition to report frankly and fearlessly, the disposition to be open to new evidence and fresh criticism. But such personal virtues can be nurtured only where they are embedded in communities and where they are reflected in institutional arrangements.

Conclusion: the nature and future of educational research

D. W. Miller entitled his contribution to the *Chronicle of Higher Education*, 6 August 1999, 'The Black Hole of Educational Research'. He refers to Diane Ravitch's check-out at a hospital and her musings

> ... what if, instead of medical researchers, I were being treated by educational researchers? ... I had a fantasy of people disagreeing about how you make a diagnosis ... arguing endlessly about whether I was even sick.

Thus, Miller argues, there is a general distrust of educational research, leading to an ignoring of whatever evidence is produced on any particular matter of policy or practice. The outside world sees endless disputes about the validity of research conclusions and even about 'how you make a diagnosis'. This suspicion permeates the minds of policy-makers and practitioners on both sides of the Atlantic, and indeed in Australia and New Zealand. It is reflected in the criticisms of research recounted in chapter 1.

These criticisms might be summarized as:

(i)   too small-scale and fragmented, constructed on different data bases, such that it is not possible to draw the 'big picture';
(ii) non-cumulative, failing to progress on the basis of previous research, for ever reinventing the wheel;
(iii) ideologically driven, serving the 'political purposes' of the researcher rather than the disinterested pursuit of the truth;
(iv) methodologically 'soft' or 'flawed', without the rigour either in the conduct of the research or in the reporting of it;
(v)   inaccessible in esoteric journals and in opaque language.

Such criticisms do, of course, apply to much research. On the other hand, there is an awful lot of the research, providing ample evidence for whatever criticism one wishes to make. The drive to publish, whatever the quality of the research, makes sure of that. However, a 'falsificationist' could quite as easily demonstrate how such general criticisms are wrong. There is good research which does address important educational issues both of policy and of professional practice. Bias and political motivation apply to the critics as much as to the researchers.

However, many of the criticisms need to be taken seriously. They raise questions about the nature of educational research which are rarely reflected upon as systematically as they need to be. Such reflection must be philosophical in nature – that is, getting clear about the object of the research, namely, 'educational practice', assessing the nature of the claims made about such 'practice' and what would count as evidence for or verification of them, showing the limitations of 'method' in researching such practices. The mode of enquiry is determined by the nature of the 'object' being enquired into.

It is tempting for those who are impatient with the fragmentary and small-scale nature of educational research, of its provisional conclusions, to look elsewhere for inspiration. The social sciences – at least certain traditions within them – seem to offer salvation. The social sciences claim to be just that – 'sciences'. Such was the inspiration and driving force, and thus the adoption of the methods and the hopes of the physical sciences. Why not a science of society? Why not, to be more specific, a science of learning or a science of teaching? Why, indeed, should not educational research in this respect be like medical research?

The analogy of medicine has, in recent years, been a powerful one, particularly the large-scale randomized controls which enable the researcher to check carefully the causal effect of particular interventions. But caution is required even about this rather selective view of medical research, let alone about the connection between such research and professional practice. The Cochrane Centre in Oxford was established precisely because of the fragmentary nature of medical research, and because the connection between such research and professional practice was tenuous indeed. But, more significantly, we need to attend much more closely to the nature of that which is being researched into. Is an 'educational practice' similar to a 'medical practice'? Clearly they are different sorts of practice, but are there sufficient likenesses such that the lessons from the one can be easily transferred to the other?

Of course, 'medical practice', and the research which might (but frequently does not) inform it, is by no means a clear concept. It includes the interactions between general practitioner and patient, as well as surgical interventions and the administration of drugs. Perhaps the interactions between doctor and patient have much in common with those between teacher and student, but even then the similarities do not take us far. A 'medical practice' has, as its purpose, the improvement of health – and built into that, of course, must be certain views about 'the good life'. Health is an evaluative as well as a descriptive concept. But an 'educational practice' is concerned with learning that which is judged to be of value – given what we believe to be of value in the cultural resources upon which the teacher draws and given what we believe to be a worthwhile form of life to pursue. Research into 'educational practice', therefore, cannot be simply a branch of the social sciences. The object of research will necessarily be seen differently by different practitioners (and by different traditions of practice within which they work) as they select different cultural resources for inspiration and different forms of life to aspire to. Educational research cannot avoid the systematic reflection upon the controversial values which pick out what is significant to study, what constitutes an educational outcome, what is to count as value added.

There is a significant philosophical tradition which constantly brings us back to the meaning and significance of an 'educational practice'. Such a tradition creates discomfort for the advocates of a social science which has little patience for the constant and often difficult task of attaining conceptual clarity. For the search for clarity leads to many distinctions, and such distinctions are an obstacle to generalization. This I have illustrated through the concept of 'learning' and 'teaching'. Failure to recognize these distinctions has led in the past to overblown theories of learning which simply do not apply in practice and are now leading us to an oversimplified science of teaching. What, instead, is required is a close philosophical examination of those key ideas which lie at the centre of 'educational practice' – learning, teaching, personal and social development, culture. Research which ignores such philosophical considerations may be research about many things. But it will not be research about 'educational practice'.

Part of that complexity, of course, lies in the nature of social reality, and attention to 'social reality' indicates the limitations of research which relies too heavily upon a scientific ideal. The social sciences provide tools for the educational researcher; they offer generalized knowledge which such a researcher must take cognizance of; but they cannot be the model of educational research. Just as (to twist a phrase from Ayer) man is not the subject of science, so educational research at its core cannot be scientific.

I have tried to explain in this book why that is the case. However, in resisting the social sciences, so have educational researchers questioned the relevance of notions such as 'truth', 'knowledge', 'objectivity', 'reality', 'causality'. In this I believe they are mistaken and have caused much harm, playing into the hands of those who wish them ill. Once one loses one's grip on 'reality', or questions the very idea of 'objectivity', or denies a knowledge-base for policy and practice, or treats facts as mere invention or construction, then the very concept of research seems unintelligible. There is a need, therefore, once again to plug educational research into that perennial (and pre-modern) philosophical tradition, and not be seduced by the postmodern embrace.

Nothing I have said should undermine the perceived relevance of the social sciences, of the need for large-scale explanatory accounts of society and of how human beings operate in and are influenced by society. Such must be the backcloth to educational thinking. The professional, struggling with the particular, will benefit from an acquaintance with the general – so long as he or she does not look to it for conclusions rather than evidence. At the heart of educational practice must be professional judgement, and that judgement needs to be informed by whatever is relevant. Educational research – understanding an educational practice – draws upon social science research. But it is something more.

This book has, therefore, endorsed the central position of the teacher as researcher. The justification lies not simply in the obvious fact that research is of little use unless it is understood and internalized by those who do the practising. It lies in the fact that the complexities of an educational practice can only be fully understood by those whose values, beliefs and understandings make it a practice of a certain sort. An 'educational practice' embodies a way of thinking about learning – its aims, what constitutes having learnt successfully, what skills, knowledge and values it is to incorporate. Such practices (and the teachers who engage in them) both draw upon public traditions which shape the practices and the thoughts of those who take part in them and, at the same time, reflect the idiosyncrasies of those participants. The teaching of history in school W by teacher X will be both the same as and different from the teaching of history in school Y by Z. There are common traditions of what history is and what counts as teaching it, as well as different traditions and different interpretations of the same traditions.

For that reason, it is difficult to see how good teaching can be separated from a research stance towards one's own teaching – a stance in which values (both public and private) about teaching are tested out in practice and in which both the values and the practice are the constant focus of reflection in the light of systematically obtained evidence.

POSTSCRIPT

The provenance of this book was the need to provide background reading for those who, though not aiming to be philosophers, wanted to think more philosophically about doing educational research. That research is so often engaged in without any knowledge of, or feeling for, the problems which can only be described as philosophical. What often is seen as a straightforward empirical matter is in fact fraught with problems – unclear concepts, questionable assumptions about verification of conclusions, naïve ideas about social facts and reality, and above all, unexamined notions of an *educational* practice. In other cases, philosophy is entered into, but often without a recognition of the complexity of the issues, as when 'positivism' becomes a 'boo-word', extended to all quantitative research, or 'postmodernism' is embraced as the final stage of philosophical evolution (there can be no post-postmodernism).

However, there is a danger. Philosophy can then become yet another bit of theory in a theoretical course – something to be learnt, made sense of and applied. Appeal is made to philosophers as authorities. 'As so-and-so says' (Foucault, Habermas, Derrida), and there ends the argument.

Philosophy should be seen as part, a major part, of teachers' and researchers' reflecting seriously on the practices they are engaged in. Philosophy begins when one feels puzzled about the meaning of what one is doing – its aims and purposes, the implicit values, the assumptions made about what is right or wrong, true or false, worthwhile or not. It is a struggle to make sense when others do not see the contradictions or unsound basis for action. And in that 'struggle to make sense', one tries to clarify what one means, finding that what previously was thought simple is really very complex. That language, when systematically reflected upon, provides a complex map of the world – physical, social and moral – which shapes how one thinks and behaves.

There are three aspects of this 'struggling to make sense' which I wish to highlight.

The first is the need to make students aware that their view of the world is not as straightforward as they think. The word 'justice' or 'fairness', for example, is used with ease, but the right kind of questioning reveals that it is not quite so simple – as Thrasymachus discovered when cross-examined by Socrates. And that probing of what one means (that search for definition through example and counter-example), skilfully applied, becomes the beginning of 'doing philosophy'.

The second aspect is that, in probing what one means, one inevitably raises questions about the nature of knowledge, what it means to be (and to become more fully) a person, what constitutes a worthwhile form of life, or how our mental activity links with a physical and social world external to ourselves. Our 'struggling to understand' can, and should be, plugged in to a 'conversation between the generations of mankind'. Our search for meaning may, at one level, be seen as a private affair, but it takes places within a public world of exploration and argument.

The third aspect is that there is no limit to the search for meaning and no easy consensus over the conclusions to be reached. Indeed, the search for understanding, the attempt to make sense and the engagement in critical reflection will rarely bring total agreement. Tolerating differences of view, but realizing that one's own conclusion can only be tentative, subject to further revision under criticism, is central to the philosophical enterprise.

And this is as true of philosophizing about education as about anything else. Reflections upon 'teaching' or 'educating' – the purposes and the most appropriate procedures to be adopted – do not take place in a vacuum. There are already practices which people, employed as teachers, are engaged in. These are picked out as educational practices. They can, of course, be engaged in rather unreflectively. Indeed, much of the preparation and training of teachers no longer encourages such critical reflection. But the person with a more philosophical spirit will reflect upon such practices and question their value and purposes. Such reflection and questioning will inevitably raise questions about what is worth learning or pursuing – the reasons why certain literature is on the syllabus or why certain subjects are optional. Before long one is into the traditional terrain of ethics, as one tries to identify the principles which justify certain activities or a certain way of life to be more worthwhile than others.

The aim, therefore, of the philosophy of education must be to get at the meanings, the assumptions, the commitments which are implicit, but too often unacknowledged, within the educational practices already engaged in. Such an 'uncovering of meaning', critically engaged in, inevitably reveals beliefs which are not sustainable or which require refining. They put the practitioners in touch with intellectual and moral traditions which give greater depth to what they are doing and which provide the basis of professional commitment, often against government or others who wish to import a more impoverished language of educational purposes.

Similarly with educational research. Here, as elsewhere, there is the constant danger of the bewitchment of the intelligence by the use of language. It is easy to stipulate a straightforward statement of aims, broken down with a finite range of measurable objectives or targets. It is relatively easy then to identify the means which, empirically, can be shown to attain these targets. It would seem to be but a matter of administrative efficiency to ensure, through various 'performance related awards' or through relevant funding 'drivers' and 'levers', that a compliant teaching force will adopt the right means to attain the right ends.

But the more philosophically minded have doubts. The aims of education embody values – a view about what is a worthwhile form of life. And such values are controversial within our society. Moreover, such controversies enter the understanding of an 'educational practice'. In 'practicing education' one is engaged in a moral enterprise as I argued in the Kolberg Lectures (Pring 2001b), and one cannot escape the subtleties of moral discussion and its roots in different moral traditions.

Select bibliography

Anderson, G. L. and Herr, K. (1999) 'The new paradigm wars: is there room for rigorous practitioner knowledge in schools and universities?'. *Educational Researcher*, **28** (5).

Atkinson, J.W. (1964) *An Introduction to Motivation*. NJ: Van Nostrand.

Ayer, A. J. (1946) *Language, Truth and Logic*. London: Penguin.

Ayer, A. J. (1956) *The Problem of Knowledge*. London: Penguin.

Ayer, A. J. (1963) *Philosophical Essays*. London: Macmillan.

Ball, S. (1981) *Beachside Comprehensive: A Case Study of Secondary Schooling*. Cambridge: Cambridge University Press.

Bassey, M. (1995) *Creating Education through Research*. Newark: Kirklington Moor Press.

Bassey, M. (1997) 'A cadre of professional researchers and a cadre of teacher researchers' (editorial). *Research Intelligence*, No. **62**, November.

Bennett, N. (1976) *Teaching Styles and Pupil Progress*. London: Open Books.

Berliner, D. C., Resnick, L. B., Cuban, L., Cole, N., Popham, W. J. and Goodlad, J. I. (eds) (1997) '"The vision thing": educational research and AERA in the 21st century, Part 2'. *Educational Researcher*, June/July.

Bhaskar, R. (1989) *Reclaiming Reality*. London: Verso.

Blunkett, D. (1999) Secretary of State's address to the annual conference of the Confederation of British Industry.

Bridges, D. (1998) 'Research for sale: moral market or moral maze'. *British Educational Research Journal*, **24** (5).

Bridges, D. (1999) 'Educational research: pursuit of truth or flight into fantasy?'. *British Educational Research Journal*, **25** (5).

Bruner, J. (1960) *The Process of Education*. Cambridge: Harvard Press.

Bruner, J. (1999) 'Postscript' in E. C. Lagemann and L. Shulman (eds) *Issues in Educational Research*. San Francisco: Jersey Bass.

Carr, D., Haldane, J., McLaughlin, T. and Pring, R. (1955) 'Return to the Crossroads: Maritain Fifty Years On'. *British Journal of Educational Studies* **43**(2).

Carr, W. (1995) *For Education*. Buckingham: Open University Press.

Carr, W. (1997) 'Professing Education in a Postmodern Age'. *Journal of Philosophy of Education*, **31** (2).

Carr, W. (2003) 'Philosophy and Education'. Unpublished Paper, University of Sheffield.

Cohen, L. and Mannion, L. (1985) *Research Methods in Education*. 2nd edn. London: Croom Helm.

Collingwood, R.G. (1946) *The Idea of History*. Oxford: Oxford University Press.

Cooley, W. W., Gage, N. L. and Scriven, M. (1997) ' "The vision thing": educational research and AERA in the 21st century'. *Educational Researcher*, May.

Dearing Report (1994) *The National Curriculum and its Assessment*. London: School Curriculum and Assessment Authority.

Dewey, J. (1916) *Democracy and Education*. New York: The Free Press.

Dewey, J. (1936) *Experience and Education*. New York: Macmillan.

Edwards, A. (2000) ' "All the evidence shows": what can reasonably be said by educational research'. *Oxford Review of Education, 26* (3,4).

Elliott, J. (1991) *Action Research for Educational Change*. Milton Keynes: Open University Press.

Elliott, J. and MacDonald, B. (eds) (1975) *People in Classrooms*. Norwich: Centre for Applied Research in Education Occasional Publications, No. 2.

Farrow, S., Tymms, P., and Henderson, B. (1999) 'Homework and attainment in primary schools'. *British Educational Research Journal, 25* (3).

Faulkner, D., Freedland, M. and Fisher, E. (1999) *Public Services: Developing approaches to governance and professionalism*. Report of a series of seminars, St John's College, Oxford.

Filmer, P. (1972) *New Directions in Sociological Theory*. London: Collier Macmillan.

Flanders, N. A. (1970) *Analysing Teachers' Behaviour*. Reading, Mass.: Addison-Wesley.

Floud, J., Halsey, A. H. and Martin, F. M. (1956) *Social Class and Educational Opportunity*. London: Heinemann.

Foster, P. (1999) ' "Never mind the quality, feel the impact": a methodological assessment of teacher research sponsored by the Teacher Training Agency'. *British Journal of Educational Studies, 41* (4).

Glaser, B. and Strauss, S. S. (1967) *The Discovery of Grounded Theory*.Chicago: Aldine.

Goldstein, H. and Myers, K. (1996) 'Freedom of information: towards a code of ethics for performance indicators'. *Research Intelligence*, No. 57.

Guba, E. G. and Lincoln, V. S. (1989) *Fourth Generation Evaluation*. London: Sage.

Gurney, P. (1980) *Behaviour Modification*. London: University of London Press.

Halsey, A. H. (1972) *Education Priority*, Vol. I. London: HMSO.

Halsey, A. H., Heath, A. F. and Ridge, J. M. (1980) *Origins and Destinations: family, class and education in modern Britain*. Oxford: Clarendon Press.

Hammersley, M. (1997) 'Educational research and teaching: a response to David Hargreaves – Teacher Training Agency Lecture'. *British Educational Research Journal, 23* (2).

Hargreaves, D. (1967) *Social Relations in a Secondary School*. London: Routledge & Kegan Paul.

Hargreaves, D. (1996) 'Teaching as a research-based profession'. Teacher

Training Agency Annual Lecture.

Hargreaves, D. (1997) 'In defence of research for evidence-based teaching'. *British Educational Research Journal*, **23** (4), 405–19.

Heath, A. F. and Clifford, P. (1990) 'Class inequalities in the twentieth century'. *Journal of the Royal Statistical Society*, Series A, 153.

Heath, A. (2000) 'The Political Arithmetic Tradition in the Sociology of Education'. *Oxford Review of Education*, **26** (3 & 4).

Hillage Report (1998) *Excellence in Research on Schools*. University of Sussex: The Institute for Employment Studies.

Hodkinson, P. (1998) *Research Intelligence*, No. 65.

Hughes-Warrington, M. (1996) 'How good an historian should I be? R. G. Collingwood on education'. *Oxford Review of Education*, Vol. 22.

Hughes-Warrington, M. (1997) 'Collingwood and the Early Paul Hirst on the forms of experience, knowledge and education'. *British Journal of Educational Studies*, Vol. 45 (2).

Kaestle, C. (1993) 'The awful reputation of education research'. *Educational Researcher*, **22** (1).

Kennedy, M. (1997) 'The connection between research and practice'. *Educational Researcher*, **26** (7).

Kirst, M. W. and Ravitch, D. (1991) *Research and the Renewal of Research*. New York: National Academy of Education.

Kohlberg, L. (1982) 'Recent work in moral education', in L. O. Ward (ed.) *The Ethical Dimension of the School Curriculum*. Swansea: Pineridge Press.

Kuhn, T. (1970) *The Structure of Scientific Revolutions*. 2nd edn. Chicago: Chicago University Press.

Lagemann, E. C. (1999) 'An auspicious moment for educational research?' in E. C. Lagemann and L. S. Shulman (eds) *Issues in Education Research*. San Francisco: Jossey-Bass Publishers.

Lortie, D. (1975) *Schoolteacher*. Chicago: University of Chicago Press.

Luntley, M. (2000) *Performance, Pay and Professionals*. London: Philosophy of Education Society of Great Britain.

Lyotard, J.-F. (1984) *The Post-modern Condition: a Report on Knowledge*. Minneapolis: University of Minneapolis Press.

Mac an Ghaill, M. (1988) *Young, Gifted and Black: Student–Teacher Relations in the Schooling of Black Youth*. Milton Keynes: Open University Press.

MacDonald, B. (1974) 'Evaluation and the control of education', in B. MacDonald and R. Walker (eds) SAFARI I *Innovation, Evaluation, Research and the Problem of Control*. Norwich: Centre for Applied Research in Education.

McCulloch, G. and Richardson, W. (2000) *Historical Research in Educational Settings*. London: Continuum.

Maritain, J. (1937) *The Degrees of Knowledge*. London: Geoffrey Bles.

Maritain, J. (1943) *Education at the Crossroads*. York: York University Press.

Mill, J.S. (1859) 'On liberty', in M. Warnock (ed.) *Utilitarianism*. London: Collins.

Miller, D.W. (1999) 'The black hole of educational research'. *Chronicle of Higher Education*, 6 August.

Mortimore, P. (1999) 'Does educational research matter?'. British Educational Research Association Presidential Address.

Mortimore, P. and Sammons, P. (1997) in J. White and M. Barber (eds) *Perspectives on School Effectiveness and School Improvement*. London: Bedford Way Papers.

Oakeshott, M. (1972) 'Education: the engagement and its frustration', in T. Fuller (ed.) *Michael Oakeshott and Education*. New Haven, CT: Yale University Press.

Oancea, A. (2003) 'Criticisms of Educational Research: Key Topics and Levels of Analysis'. Paper given at the BERA Conference, September.

O'Connor, D. J. (1956) *An Introduction to the Philosophy of Education*. London: Routledge & Kegan Paul.

Ormerod, P. (1998) *Butterfly Economics*. London: Faber & Faber.

Peshkin, A. (1978) *Growing Up American: Schooling and the Survival of Community*. Chicago: University of Chicago Press.

Peters, R. S. (1965) *Ethics and Education*. London: George Allen and Unwin.

Peters, R. S. (1974) *Psychology and Ethical Development*. London: Unwin.

Petrosino, A. J., Rounding, C., McDonald, S. and Chalmers, I. (1999) *Improving Systematic Reviews of Evaluations*, paper presented for meeting on Research Synthesis and Public Policy, University College London, 15/16 July.

Popper, K. (1959) *The Logic of Scientific Discovery*. Oxford: Oxford University Press.

Popper, K. (1972) *Objective Knowledge: an evolutionary approach*. Oxford: Oxford University Press.

Power, C. and Reimer, J. (1978) 'Moral atmosphere', in W. Damon (ed.) *New Directions for Child Development and Moral Development*. San Francisco: Jossey-Bass.

Pring, R. (2000) 'False dualisms: quantitative and qualitative research'. *Journal of Philosophy of Education*, **34** (3).

Pring, R. (2001a) 'The Virtues and Vices of an Educational Researcher'. *Journal of Philosophy of Education*, Special Issue.

Pring, R. (2001b) 'Education as a Moral Practice'. *Journal of Moral Education*, **30** (2).

Putnam, R. T. and Borko, H. (2000) 'What do new views of knowledge and thinking have to say about research on teacher learning?'. *Educational Researcher*, **29** (1).

Reynolds, D. (1998) 'Teacher Effectiveness: Better Teachers, Better Schools'. *Research Intelligence*, No. 66.

Rutter Report (1979) *Fifteen Thousand Hours: Secondary Schools and Effects on Children*. London: Open Books.

Ryan, A. (1997) *John Dewey and the High Tide of American Liberalism*. New York: W. W. Norton.

Ryle, G. (1954) *Dilemmas*. Cambridge: Cambridge University Press.

Scheffler, I. (1965) *Conditions of Knowledge*. Chicago: Scott. Foresman.

Schön, D. (1995) *The Reflective Practitioner*. London: Arena.

Schutz, A. (1964) 'The Stranger', in A. Brodersen (ed.) *Studies in Social Theory*. The Hague: Martinus Nijhoff.

Schutz, A. (1972) *The Phenomenology of the Social World*. London: Heinemann.

Simons, H. (1981) *Towards a Science of the Singular*. Norwich: University of East Anglia.

Simons, H. (1995) 'The politics and ethics of educational research in England: contemporary issues'. *British Educational Research Journal*, **21** (4).

Stenhouse, L. (1967) *Culture and Education*. London: Nelson.

Stenhouse, L. (1975) *An Introduction to Curriculum Research and Development*. London: Heinemann.

Stronach, I. and MacLure, P. (1997) *Educational Research Undone: the postmodern embrace*. Buckingham: Open University Press.

Sylva, K. and Hurry, J. (1995) *The Effectiveness of Reading Recovery and Phonological Training for Children with Reading Problems*. London: Thomas Coram Research Unit.

Taylor, C. (1989) *Sources of the Self*. Cambridge: Cambridge University Press.

Teacher Training Agency (1996) 'Teaching as a Research-based Profession'. London: TTA.

Thomas, G. and Pring, R. (2004) (eds) *Evidence based Educational Practice*, Milton Keynes: Open University Press.

Tooley, J. and Darby, D. (1998) *Educational Research: an OFSTED Critique*. London: OFSTED.

Toulmin, S. (1972) *Human Understanding*. Oxford: Clarendon Press.

Wilson, J. (1979) *Preface to the Philosophy of Education*. London: Routledge & Kegan Paul.

Wilson, P. (1967) *Interest and Discipline in Education*. London: Routledge & Kegan Paul.

Winch, P. (1958) *The Idea of a Social Science*. London: Routledge & Kegan Paul.

Winch, P. (1972) 'Understanding a Primitive Society', in P. Winch (ed.) *Ethics and Action*. London: Routledge & Kegan Paul.

Woods, P. (1979) *The Divided School*. London: Routledge & Kegan Paul.

Woozley, A. D. (1949) *Theory of Knowledge*. London: Hutchinson.

Young, M. F. D. (1972) *Knowledge and Control*. London: Methuen.

Index

AG 06

For enquiries or renewal at
Ardleigh Green LRC
Tel: 01708 455011 Ext: 2040